If you want to reach our wor[...] *Greater Glory* is a must-read [...] stories, confronted with Biblical truth, and convicted to join with other believers and ministries inside and outside my tribe in fulfilling the Great Commission. After reading *Greater Glory*, I have a greater desire to be a part of God's plan: bringing life to a dying world through His loving church.

—Stan Grant
Lead Pastor
Cloverhill Church, Midlothian, VA

This book comes at a critical time in our history. We live in a challenging time, and people are searching for answers. But sadly, many of them are not looking to the church. Why? If we're honest, it's because sometimes what they see inside the church doesn't look any different than what they're already experiencing. This book addresses critical issues, such as forgiveness, resolving conflict, tearing down walls, unity, and others. I pray that you will read it with others and look for ways to address the great needs of our day.

—David Ludwig
Associate Director of Church Health
Baptist Resource Network of Pennsylvania/South Jersey

In his book *Greater Glory*, Bob Santos diagnoses our condition and answers with the solution for a vibrant church in a fallen world. As he states, "Our fractured and dying world desperately needs a unified church to rise." Bob has captured the spirit and intent of the church that Jesus loves and gave His life for. He accomplishes this by critically dividing Scripture, with a mature observation from experience, to foster unity across the body of Christ. We heed God's call to demonstrate His love to the world through our love for each other.

—Bob Jeannot
Lead Pastor, New Wine Community Church
Executive Leader, Kingdom Connection Network
Greater Detroit Metropolitan Area, MI

Bob Santos' *Greater Glory* is the best antidote yet to the divisive colloquies of the Christian faith. Bob deftly addresses ways that we can bridge spiritual, racial, cultural, and relational gaps through sound Biblical theology and application. Making a compelling case for kingdom building in the 21st century, Bob shows us how we can wisely employ keys that unlock the transformational power of unity. As you read through this book, you will discover how you can be part of bringing heaven to earth. I eagerly await this book's impact on the body of Christ and beyond!

—Ryan E. Faison, M.Div.
Campus Pastor
Christ Church, Clifton, NJ

Bob brings to light the vital importance of the Christian unity that Jesus prays for His church in John 17, as well as the blessings that we can have as churches in a community functioning as part of a larger body. He not only does this in theological terms, but also helps us to practice unity and navigate some of the challenges that churches can have as we seek to live in unity in light of Jesus' prayer. This book is very timely as Christians and churches seem to be divided, mostly over non-kingdom issues. May the truths that Bob writes about, be evident in our lives and church families.

—Rob Sparr
Lead Pastor
Graystone Evangelical Presbyterian Church, Indiana, PA

One of the most difficult focuses in the local church is unity. How can a church live in unity together, and beyond that, have unity with other churches? I believe other churches are not competition, but a completion in fulfilling what God desires. *Greater Glory* takes a dive into building bridges and navigating the tensions to unite and not divide the Christian church. Bob gives great practical advice and wonderful reflections with each chapter to dig deeper.

—Keith Rowell
Campus Pastor
Thrive Church, North Chesterfield, VA

Greater Glory

THE TRANSFORMATIONAL POWER OF CHRISTIAN UNITY

Greater Glory

THE TRANSFORMATIONAL POWER OF CHRISTIAN UNITY

SfMe Media
A Growing Adventure

BOB SANTOS

SEARCH FOR ME MINISTRIES, INC.
INDIANA, PA

Greater Glory: The Transformational Power of Christian Unity
By Bob Santos

Published by SfMe Media
A Division of Search for Me Ministries, Inc.
www.sfme.org

Printed in the United States of America

Library of Congress Control Number: 2022950982

ISBN: 978-1-937956-32-5
EPUB ISBN: 978-1-937956-33-2

CONTENTS

Introduction

---◆---

Do you ever fret about the future? Do you ever feel alone in an increasingly automated and impersonal world? Are you dissatisfied with the direction of the government? Have you found yourself mystified by the moral unraveling of society? Do you worry about how the world will look for your children or grandchildren?

If you answered "yes" to any of these questions, you are not alone. Sometimes, the pace of life feels like we are driving through an old neighborhood at high speed. Fleeting glimpses of more stable times make hope for a better tomorrow seem elusive.

What promise does our world have for real change? Will it come through academics? Not much there gives us cause to rejoice. How about politics? Talk about frustration and futility! The business world? Greed abounds with but a few scattered bright spots. And media? Objective news reporting, it seems, is a long-lost relic buried in an old trunk sitting in a corner of the attic.

What about the *church*? Do you see the church as the primary source of meaningful change in our nation? Though our practice of Christianity often seems like a mess, God has a plan—He always has a plan—to bring life to a dying world through His living church. Potential abounds, and we already have much in place.

For my part, I have spent much of the past decade writing books to address niche areas of spiritual growth that are either widely misunderstood or get too little attention among Christians. How exciting it is to help people mature and grow spiritually healthy! With this book, I want to expand my scope beyond the individual and tackle a topic that possesses huge potential for positive change: *the unity of the church.*

As you will read in the first chapter, many years ago the Lord put His finger on my heart and transformed my perspective of Christian relationships. I hope He uses this book to do something similar in your life.

Meaningful change rarely comes easily, though. Many of the concepts related to unity present significant challenges for us. And no single person or book can adequately address every facet of such a deep-rooted problem as division among Christians. We can, however, choose to take deliberate steps in a healthy direction.

Today's church faces many daunting challenges, but the future is by no means dark for the people of God. The Lord has a "secret weapon" to overcome the tide of evil that appears to be rising in our world: *His unified body of believers*. As we return to the basic elements of Christian unity, we will chart a fresh course for transformational ministry in our increasingly broken world.

CHAPTER ONE

WHOSE KINGDOM ARE YOU BUILDING?

◆

"But seek first His kingdom and His righteousness, and all these things will be provided to you."

Matthew 6:33 (NASB)

If you have not chosen the kingdom of God first, it will in the end make no difference what you choose instead.

—William Law

I cannot say that my impressions of Christians were very favorable prior to enrolling at a state university. I knew many people who attended church regularly, but other than involvement in a local congregation, not much distinguished the average churchgoer from the ones who avoided those hallowed doors.

Only rarely did my own feet cross the threshold of a church building. I was no saint; that is certain. Still, neither was I morally worse than many of the professing people of faith I knew. A few devoted individuals provided refreshing exceptions, but personal faith seemed mostly irrelevant in the public sphere. Spiritually speaking, I cannot remember looking at many individuals in our community and thinking, "I wish I had what that person has." If ever there was jealousy on my part, it was over money, appearance, or athletic ability. "Religion" was something that people did; few visible traces of spiritual life could be seen.

Attending college brought a different experience, providing far more diversity than I had experienced growing up. Yes, there were professing Christians who seemed like oddities in the mix of a secular university, but others presented something more. That "more" attracted me, and by my second year I was poring over the pages of the Bible, trying to make sense of it all.

The story is too long for this context, but exploring a trail of Scriptural truth led me to surrender my life to God and ask Jesus to be my Lord and Savior. Not long after, I was water baptized back in my hometown by a local pastor. Thus began a lifelong journey of walking with God and seeking to serve His purposes.

Uncertainty and upheaval marked those early years of my Christian walk, but there was also something near mystical about the experience—especially regarding my involvement in campus ministry. Pastors and leaders from various churches took it upon themselves to invest in the lives of college students, and I was one of the welcoming recipients. My faith sprouted quickly.

DEEP DISAPPOINTMENT

About ten years after graduation, I found myself struggling to navigate life in that same college community. I was married to a wonderful Christian woman (Debi). We lived with our two adorable kids in a small home in a nice neighborhood. I was also heavily involved in our local fellowship, which included serving for six years on the church board.

My experiences with the "underbelly" of church life no doubt contributed to a crisis of faith that conflicted my heart. Although my devotion to Christ never seriously wavered during that difficult season, a deep sense of disappointment permeated my soul and caused me to flounder in my Christian walk. Contributing to my struggle was the feeling that my service to God was a miserable failure. Rather than reaching souls and fostering transformation, I felt we were trying to pacify immature, self-centered adults who had been in the church for much of their lives.

I did not sign up to put out "brush fires" or keep people pacified, so I jumped quickly when the opportunity arose for Debi and me to work with our church's college ministry. Our own campus fellowship experience had been life changing, and going back to those roots seemed like the Lord's leading.

A NEW OPPORTUNITY

Even as my mind filled with visions of changing the world, yet another shadow of disappointment settled into my heart. Before Debi and I stepped into leadership, about twenty students had involved themselves with the campus group's activities. I felt much like Gideon as that number dropped to around five before we even got started. And no matter what we did, the numbers did not increase.

I continued to work hard regardless. At times, the challenges seemed insurmountable—I was also holding down a full-time job and trying to care for my young family. Even so, I knew I was following God's leading and moving in the right direction.

Facing a barrier beyond our abilities, we enlisted the help of intercessors from our church. Before each weekly student meeting, several devoted prayer warriors would come to intercede for the university and for us. We also held multiple outreaches to gather students we could disciple to become faithful laborers for Christ. But no matter how hard we tried, nothing went according to our expectations.

That first year of campus ministry felt fruitless, as though we were working in vain. Still, I held tightly to the hope that a new school year would bring new students to increase the size of our group. It did not. Instead, we seemed to go backward rather than forward. My frustrations mounted.

I still hold strong memories of a particular week in October of that second year. The night of our fellowship meeting proved especially disappointing. Only one of our intercessors attended the pre-service gathering, and even she struggled to get there. "I'm not sure what happened this week," our faithful prayer partner explained. "I felt suicidal, and that never happens to me. I came out tonight only because I was determined not to let the devil win."

That evening's campus ministry meeting fared no better. Instead of our usual six students, we had three. And of that three, only one genuinely engaged with my message. I felt as though we had slammed head-on into an immovable wall. No doubt, my memory of that night reflects as one of the lowest points in our sixteen-plus years of campus ministry.

AN UNEXPECTED EXPERIENCE

At about that time, God did something unexpected. I mean, *really* unexpected. Some people do not believe that the Lord speaks to Christians except through the Bible. Well, He spoke to me. And I cannot say that I welcomed His words, at least not initially.

The setting was typical during that season of my life. I had gone before the Lord to petition His blessings on our ministry efforts. It was then that the Holy Spirit spoke unthinkable (from my perspective) words to me: "I want you to pray for Campus Crusade."

The voice was not audible, but it came clearly through my mind nonetheless. I instinctively knew that God was directing me to pray His blessings over our local chapter of Campus Crusade for Christ (now known as Cru). The problem—at least in my eyes— was that Campus Crusade's fellowship meetings were much larger than ours. In fact, well over a hundred students came out for their weekly meetings that were held in the largest room of the student union. We usually had six or less in attendance, resembling a small tribe of misfits more than a world-changing army.

My response to God in that moment? I scoffed. "Yeah, right, Lord. What's wrong with this picture?" The very idea of praying for Him to bless such a large group seemed inconceivable in light of our twenty-two-month struggle to grow our little band. What happened next would change me forever.

Instead of consoling me or comforting my struggling heart, the Lord responded with another question: "Whose kingdom are you building, yours or Mine?" And not only was the Holy Spirit speaking, He was also opening my eyes. I felt as though a curtain had been pulled back to expose the self-absorbed motives of my heart. Sure, I was seeking to build God's kingdom on earth, but in that instant, I realized there was also a whole lot of *ME* in the mix.

Nearly my entire sense of significance had been wrapped up in finding ministry success. And if I were to fail at what matters most in life, my existence would forever be defined by the shame I had felt throughout much of my childhood. Sadly, I was trying to build my own kingdom in God's name. It was the only way for me to feel good about an inferior life—or so I thought during that early stage of my Christian walk.

CHANGES

That revealing prayer experience changed me forever. When confronted by the Lord about the ugly truth of my motives, I repented immediately. Not only did I begin to pray for Campus Crusade, I also determined I would never again build my own kingdom in Christ's name. Certainly, I had a stewardship to fulfill with our group, but the grand purpose of my life would no longer be just about the work that *I* was doing.

Not long after that watershed moment, our group began to grow. The attendance quickly jumped into the double digits, and never dropped back. And while prayer had been a near-constant focus, outward changes in our ministry efforts took place only *after* the Lord had worked an inward change in me.

I also began to network with the other campus ministers. Together, we held joint worship events as a collective Christian community. We began to call ourselves "The River," meaning many streams coming together as one. Challenges were common, and our efforts were by no means seamless, but the Lord blessed richly nonetheless.

During those campus ministry years, I also developed Bible study materials I felt needed to go to a broader audience. And so we launched Search for Me Ministries, Inc., with a vision to help form and equip a generation of world-changers for Christ. The mode of ministry changed, but a kingdom vision continued to drive my labors.

In a way that only God could orchestrate, our new ministry obtained a house across the street from the university. After renovating the garage into a meeting room, I invited the campus ministers to join me for weekly prayer meetings. We also began to provide an annual welcome-back luncheon for the group. A delicious picnic meal and lively fellowship would be followed by a short devotion through which I shared about the importance of Christian unity.

It took nearly a decade, but the "kingdom culture" eventually caught on. A special moment came one year as we enjoyed our annual picnic lunch together. The campus minister turnout was great, and I gave the ministry veterans an opportunity to share with the rookies. As they took turns speaking, I realized my customary message about unity would not be necessary. The campus ministry veterans had said it all!

The process has not been without struggle, but as a whole, that campus ministry environment continues to be noncompetitive. Many of those ministers have become friends, and they often discuss plans before holding outreaches or major events. Several even banded together for a weekly large group meeting, while still maintaining their own small group identities. How refreshing it has been, but the story does not end there.

ANOTHER KINGDOM OPPORTUNITY

One day, I received a letter from a retired Methodist minister (who was new to our community) advertising a "clergy fellowship" lunch. I ignored it. Another letter came the following month, and I reluctantly decided to check it out.

Those attending felt drawn together, and as we began to explore the possibilities, two themes became apparent. First, if we were going to sacrifice precious time to participate in a monthly meeting, the group needed to be *Christ centered*. There would be no room for a "believe what you want" mentality. Our fellowship gatherings would be built on Biblical truth, or they would not happen at all.

Second, *prayer* would be a primary focus. Yes, we wanted to get to know one another and build relationships, but we did not want the group to be just about us. Later, when a passionate Lutheran pastor brought a video about pastors praying together, we all jumped to say, "That's what we want to be about!"

Before long, friendships began to develop, as walls between pastors fell. Community prayer meetings eventually followed, and the "spiritual tide" in our county began to rise. Testimonies about God's work became common, and those in surrounding areas began to take notice.

I found it especially rewarding to see the influence of these united efforts on young people. In an era when so many of our youth seem to be abandoning the Christian faith, we were blessed to see them drawn in by the fellowship, love, and prayers of older believers.

PERSPECTIVE

I share a little of my story to provide some necessary perspective. I know I am presenting an ideal as I write about the importance of Christian unity, but something more than an ideal is involved.

Christianity is not failing in America. Instead, Christians have largely failed to advance God's kingdom because we have been focused on our own feudal states. All too often, we lament the demise of our nation while failing to realize how a divided church contributes to the problem. We have long ignored key Biblical principles regarding Christian unity, and for that we are paying a steep price.

Some have sought to remedy national moral decay through political action. And while I believe Christians should involve themselves in just about every area of society, I also understand that politics will divide us further if we embrace worldly mindsets rather than a heart of Christian love.

Real change will happen only as we return to our roots. Only as we build upon a solid Biblical foundation can we truly advance God's kingdom in this broken world. That foundation most certainly involves the people of God being joined together in unity through the bond of love.

The idea of Christian unity might seem like an impossibility to some, but the Lord is indeed doing such a work in our day. Over the past couple of decades, I have watched walls between believers come down and the kingdom of God go forward in practical ways. The transformation might not be as widespread as we would like, but it is happening. And how we need a day when unity among believers becomes the norm and not the exception!

REFLECTION

1. How do you think God views the concept of Christian unity?

2. Can you identify an area of your life in which you are serving yourself in God's name?

3. How does division affect the church's ability to influence our nation for good? Are there ways in which you are contributing to that division?

CHAPTER TWO

WHY UNITY MATTERS

◆

And knowing their thoughts, Jesus said to them, "Every kingdom divided against itself is laid waste; and no city or house divided against itself will stand."
Matthew 12:25 (NASB)

Satan always hates Christian fellowship; it is his policy to keep Christians apart. Anything which can divide saints from one another he delights in. He attaches far more importance to godly intercourse than we do. Since union is strength, he does his best to promote separation.
—Charles Spurgeon

When reading the Bible, we tend to brush over uncomfortable topics, or we try to conform them to our perspectives. I am well aware of this bias within me, so I do my best to let the truth of Scripture speak for itself. Spiritual truths are not always pleasant to the taste, but they nourish the soul. Such can certainly be the case when addressing the issue of Christian unity.

The theme of unity is central to New Testament teaching, but I have seen many of God's people give it little regard. The call for unity applies both *within* and *between* churches, but is easy to ignore because of the many challenges involved. All too often, church attenders proclaim just cause to excuse their failure to love and honor others within a congregation. Virtually all pastors champion the importance of unity—as long as it is within their own spheres. Yet when considering the body of Christ at large, the story often differs.

Pastors preach unity to their congregations because they understand well the difficulties of leading a divided church. But how often do they lift up their heads and look outward to gain a broader perspective of the Lord's work on this earth? Sadly, some leaders embrace attitudes and actions toward "outsiders" that they would never think of allowing within their own spheres.

The Lord's perspective is so much broader than ours. In proclaiming Himself to be the good shepherd, Jesus said:

> "And I have other sheep that are not of this fold; I must bring them also, and they will listen to My voice; and they will become one flock, with one shepherd." John 10:16 (NASB)

One flock, with one shepherd. Jesus does not separate Baptist, Presbyterian, or Pentecostal flocks. Nor does He identify native, black, or white sheep. Designations such as rich versus poor or educated versus uneducated have no bearing in heaven's eyes. Nor does God favor a US congregation over a gathering in Columbia, Iran, or Zimbabwe.

The Lord sees His sheep as a *single* flock, meaning there are not many separate churches in a community, but rather *one* church with many different expressions. Each is designed by God to serve kingdom purposes in conjunction with the others.

As I highlight four primary reasons for the importance of Christian unity, I encourage you to think beyond the scope of your church affiliation and consider how these principles apply to the body of Christ within your community. I am not referring to a kind of ecumenical approach that makes Biblical doctrine an afterthought (we will address the issue of doctrine soon enough), but rather one rooted in a *new covenant relationship* with Jesus Christ.

1. Unity strengthens; division weakens. Genesis 11 tells the story of the *Tower of Babel*. The people of Shinar had come together to build an idolatrous tower to heaven. What did God think about their joint endeavor?

The Lord said, "Behold, they are one people, and they all have the same language. And this is what they began to do, and now nothing which they purpose to do will be impossible for them." Genesis 11:6

These people were enemies of God, exalting themselves against the throne of heaven. Yet the Lord recognized the power of their unity. How much more dynamic are the people of God when they come together as one?

Jesus spoke bluntly about our need for unity in the Holy Spirit:

"Every kingdom divided against itself is laid waste; and no city or house divided against itself will stand." Matthew 12:25b (NASB)

These words proclaim a powerful reality, and they were spoken by our Lord Himself. When we are divided, the kingdom of darkness gains ground in its quest to destroy. Even so, far too many Christians live contrary to this message. We satisfy ourselves with shallow excuses for our divisions. "Their doctrine isn't as solid as ours." Or, "They don't worship the right way." Or, "I went there once, and no one greeted me."

Throughout history, the church has at times been the most influential force in culture. Family, community, and even government stability were all wrapped up in church life. Sadly, much of that influence has been squandered to the point of irrelevancy. I am sure we could identify several causes for this tragic loss of influence in human lives, but our divisiveness must be near the top of the list. Divided Christians look much like the average churchgoers I encountered during my high school years. Other than a professed belief in God, not much distinguishes them from the rest of society.

As we bicker and fight, hell advances. Hopelessness increases. Violent people rise. Addictions multiply. Families fray at the seams. Fears reign. Far-flung ideas become cultural truth. Where godly influence is absent, darkness reigns. But how can the Lord's people stem the tide of evil in this world when roots of darkness entangle our own hearts?

A divided church will also squander precious resources. In how many ways could churches complement each other instead of trying to reproduce the same efforts to accomplish the same basic mission?

If the people of Shinar showed so much potential for evil in their unity, how much more good can the people of God accomplish together under the banner of Christ?

2. We alienate our children when we are divided. Instead of reflecting the love of God as esteemed in the Scriptures, Christians often get caught up—both within and between our churches—with petty differences and squabbles. And while our eyes are fixed on getting our own way, the eyes of our young people spy the hypocrisy of shallow love.

From before they could walk, we taught our kids about God's goodness and His great love for humanity. Time and time again, we exhorted them to follow the "Golden Rule" by doing to others as they would have others do to them. So, when young people see the opposite at work in us, they instinctively question the validity of our faith and the message we preach. Sometimes, they even question the existence of God.

In speaking to His disciples, Jesus set a new standard for love from which *no one* is exempt:

"I am giving you a new commandment, that you love one another; just as I have loved you, that you also love one another. By this all people will know that you are My disciples: if you have love for one another." John 13:34–35 (NASB)

The church's lack of unity bleeds hypocrisy. And because of it, we have lost our voice to influence the next generation of youth. That absence has opened the door for all kinds of foolish ideas to flourish. Ideologies that make older Christians shake their heads in disbelief are now considered normal by many of today's young people.

If we want to reverse the tide and see the church exert cultural influence, it will not happen through trendy worship, cool stage sets, or passionate political campaigning. Nor will "fire and brimstone" sermons or public criticisms bring change. We can criticize them all we want, but today's youth find relevance in *authenticity* as they watch older adults genuinely seeking to live out the ideals of Scripture. *If we want to recover our voice with young people, we must recover the love that God compels us to have for our brothers and sisters in Christ.*

3. We alienate the unsaved when we are divided. This third issue is similar to the second, but with a different sphere of people. We can glean much from Jesus' High Priestly Prayer that He lifted to the heavenly Father just before going to the cross:

"The glory which You have given Me I have given to them, that they may be one, just as We are one; I in them and You in Me, that they may be perfected in unity, so that the world may know that You sent Me, and loved them, even as You have loved Me." John 17:22–23

Many churches emphasize winning souls to Christ, and rightly so. Unfortunately, our actions too often conflict with the gospel message we preach. With our mouths we tell non-Christians to join us in pursuing Christ, but our lack of Christian love sends a conflicting message.

I am by no means new to church life. Before relocating, Debi and I were active members of the same local fellowship for almost forty years. Throughout my life, I have also worked closely with other pastors and churches. If I were to give an honest appraisal, I would say that unity between Christian churches in a community is the exception and not the norm. Yet the opposite should be true.

We can bemoan the negative trends in our world, but until we live what we preach, until we learn to truly walk in Christ's love, our message to the unsaved will ring hollow. If we genuinely care about those lost in sin, we will not ignore the widespread division that eats at our mission like a cancer.

Jesus' High Priestly Prayer presents an ideal to strive for, yet it is more than an ideal. Our Lord truly expects His people to be unified. Why else would He have lifted such a profound request before the Father's throne?

Through the words recorded in John 13:34–35 and 17:22–23, Jesus' disciples recognized His emphasis on the importance of love-based unity. Why did our Lord make such a point as He prepared them for His sacrificial death and subsequent departure from earth? In our world, there is nothing like genuine unity. Division is the norm because people naturally bicker, hold grudges, and vie for control. *Christianity, according to God's design, is anything but natural.*

Now, you might say, "Well, Bob, it's really hard for me to love all other Christians. I mean, you probably haven't met some of the church people I know!" You might be surprised.

Of course it is difficult! Unity requires a higher level of living—and of loving. And that is exactly what reveals our unseen God. The church is not merely a noble, civic-minded organization. *We are the church of the living God, the body of Christ born from above through an imperishable seed* (1 Peter 1:22–23).

If our Lord's glory is not displayed by the church, we lose a core element of our witness. And nowhere does that glory shine more than through our relationships with one another.

Genuine love and unity capture people's attention. Innately, they realize something "otherworldly" is at work. And when our treatment of one another meshes with the salvation message we preach, hearts are drawn to heaven's King.

What is it we all want? We want our Lord to be glorified and His kingdom advanced. We want people to turn from darkness to embrace the kingdom of light. We want to see souls saved, families healed, and violent hearts redeemed.

If we truly care about the unsaved, we will love one another. If we refuse to walk in love, we will corrupt and pollute our witness. And those outside the camp of Biblical Christianity will use our failure to justify their rejection of the Lord. Yes, they will be accountable to God, but do you really want to fan the flames of deception and rebellion against heaven's King?

Make no mistake; disunity undermines the spiritual authority of the church to influence her surrounding culture.

4. Our Lord passionately desires our unity. The importance of Christian unity is more than a theological concept. *Unity provides a reflection of our heavenly Father's loving heart.* Having raised two children into adulthood, and having worked with young people for many years, I think I can at least begin to fathom the essence of God's desires.

As a father, I take special joy when our adult children love one another. Watching them sit at the holiday table joking and laughing while playing a board game warms my heart like nothing else.

Where does such a desire for unity originate? It is a reflection of our Father's love that most parents—regardless of their faith tradition—embrace. Through family, God has given us a glimpse into His own heart. I know that many wounded souls in the West proclaim the abusive nature of "patriarchy." Too often, though, they use the shortcomings of men to malign our heavenly Father whose heart beats with love like no other!

Think, for a minute, about the *Trinity*—Father, Son, and Holy Spirit. The great mystery of *Three in One* reveals something powerful about the nature of God. The Father, Son, and Holy Spirit are One, bound together by perfect love. This means our God is passionate about oneness. And because He created us in His image with the capacity to love, He desires that we be unified as well. Let us return to Jesus' High Priestly Prayer:

"I am no longer in the world; and yet they themselves are in the world, and I come to You. Holy Father, keep them in Your name, the name which You have given Me, that they may be one even as We are." John 17:11

"I do not ask on behalf of these alone, but for those also who believe in Me through their word; that they may all be one; even as You, Father, are in Me and I in You, that they also may be in Us, so that the world may believe that You sent Me." John 17:20–21

"The glory which You have given Me I have given to them, that they may be one, just as We are one; I in them and You in Me, that they may be perfected in unity, so that the world may know that You sent Me,

and loved them, even as You have loved Me." John
17:22–23

Any knowledgeable teacher of God's Word will tell you that
repetition in the Bible carries a special weight. So here, just
before sacrificing His life for our sins, Jesus wraps up the final
teaching session with His disciples by lifting a special prayer to
heaven. Not once, but *three* times, He prays for His people to
be unified. Also, *twice* Jesus mentions the effect that Christian
love and unity will have on the surrounding world.

These verses need little commentary; our Lord's desire is clear.
The most significant questions do not involve the meaning of
Jesus' prayer, but rather our response to it.

What does it mean to proclaim we are "Christians"—followers
of Christ? Do we do it for Him or for ourselves? How deeply
do we care about our Lord's desires? How much do we value
the price of His suffering on our behalf? Do we care enough to
let go of an offense? To forgive when expectations go unmet?
To reach across denominational boundaries with a hand of
fellowship?

We all have selfish tendencies. We all have times when we
are jealous of "more successful" believers. And many of us
have even been deeply hurt by other Christians. Too often,
coldness, bitterness, and hardened hearts follow.

I am not presenting you with mere wishful thoughts. I myself
have been wounded by people of God. I have felt the piercing
pain of a stab in the back from a brother who should have
had my back. No, those incidents of "friendly fire" should not
have happened. But they did. And I was compelled to choose
a response. In the end, the love of God won out. Church pain
runs deep, so it did not happen easily or quickly, but in time I
learned to forgive and let go.

If we, the children of God who have both His Word and His Spirit, cannot effectively live out the love of God, who can? If we cannot forgive and embrace one another in unity, who in our world will? Who will give our children and grandchildren hope that sacred oneness is even possible?

The power to exercise such a depth of love might be beyond our human ability, but it is not beyond the God who dwells within us and empowers us to love. That is why Jesus spoke the way He did. "By this all people will know that you are My disciples: if you have love for one another" (John 13:35, NASB).

If we truly desire to honor our Lord and Savior, we will honor His desire for the unity of His people. I am not saying that it is easy to live out such a high standard of love, but by drawing upon God's empowering grace, it is possible.

Why is our Christian unity important? A kingdom divided cannot stand. Our children need to see authentic Christianity in action. A dying world longs to see the love of God revealed. And, as important as anything else, our Lord deeply desires that we be of one heart and mind as His beloved children.

Our unity matters. It matters to the powers of darkness. It matters to our children. It matters to those who stand on the precipice of hell. And it matters to the eternal King who rescued us from the pit of despair. But does it matter to us?

REFLECTION

1. Please read Matthew 12:25b. How does this statement apply to the church?

2. How does Christian unity testify of God's goodness?

3. How does disunity undermine our Christian witness?

Chapter Three
Defining Unity

Beyond all these things put on love, which is the perfect bond of unity.

Colossians 3:14

Believers are never told to become one; we already are one and are expected to act like it.

—Joni Eareckson Tada

We are only beginning the third chapter, but I am sure I have prompted some questions. Perhaps you are thinking about situations in which unity seems impossible. Or maybe you are waiting for me to proclaim the need for unity at all costs, regardless of doctrinal beliefs. These are issues I have had to work through myself, so I find it necessary to explain more fully what I mean by "Christian unity."

From a New Testament perspective, unity speaks of a *oneness* of heart, mind, and spirit. Rather than exploring a single definition, however, we will consider a *mindset* as communicated by the apostle Paul in his letter to the Philippian church:

Therefore if there is any encouragement in Christ, if there is any consolation of love, if there is any fellowship of the Spirit, if any affection and compassion, make my joy complete by being of the same mind, maintaining the same love, united in spirit, intent on one purpose.

> Do nothing from selfishness or empty conceit, but with humility of mind regard one another as more important than yourselves; do not merely look out for your own personal interests, but also for the interests of others. Philippians 2:1–4

Paul's reference to unity in this passage encompasses seven basic elements:

1. Being of the same mind
2. Maintaining the same love
3. Being united in spirit
4. Being intent on one purpose
5. Doing nothing from empty glory or self-conceit
6. Regarding one another as more important than ourselves
7. Looking out for the interests of others

Paul wrote this letter to exhort a specific church—the one in Philippi—but it would be unwise to limit our perspective to such a small group of people. Yes, his epistle was written within a specific context, but the principles of unity are universal. They apply to the *entire* body of Christ. With perhaps the exception of the Thessalonians—who seemed to excel in their love for one another—Paul somehow appealed for unity in every church he addressed by letter.

Pondering Philippians 2:1-4 compels me to pause and ask questions. Do we carry such a mindset when thinking about others who attend our church? And what about believers who are outside the sphere of our local church or denomination? If we do not think of them as esteemed members of the body of Christ, we must ask why. Is it because we feel we have special permission from God to hold dark feelings toward those who disagree with the entirety of our religious practice or doctrine?

UNITY VERSUS UNIFORMITY

Unity and *uniformity* are two very different concepts, but we often confuse them. Allow me to explain.

Christian unity is rooted in a *new covenant* relationship with God. Unfortunately, the Western world—including much of the church—has strayed far from the covenantal mindset with which the Bible was penned. *A covenant is a sacred and binding relationship of the highest order.*[1] Vestiges of covenantal thinking still remain (think wedding ceremony), but they serve mostly as decorations in modern societies.

People sometimes confuse *contracts* with *covenants*, which is a huge mistake. In producing a contract, each party is concerned primarily about its *own* interests. But with a relational covenant, we emphasize the *other party's* interests. Consider marriage vows, for example. When a couple exchanges vows at the altar, you will not hear a bride or groom say, "I stand here today thinking mainly of myself and pursuing what's best for me. I promise to stay with you as long as it is to my benefit." No! Marriage vows are intended to be *sacred* covenant vows, pledging to honor and seek the well-being of a new husband or wife.

Becoming a Christian is never about elevating our personal interests. Does not the call to repentance address our motivations in this regard? When we repent, we cease to put ourselves first and begin to elevate God's interests above our own. And God's interests involve people—especially His children.

The concept of covenant is the closest thing we have to the faithful relationship between the Father, Son, and Holy Spirit. And, Biblically speaking, covenants are *family* affairs. If you enter into a covenant relationship with the Lord, and I enter into a covenant relationship with the Lord, by God's design we join together in a sacred bond. We become the family of God, *blood brothers and sisters* bound together in love through Jesus Christ.

---

1. For a more thorough examination of this topic, please consider my book *Drinking Truth: Embracing the Covenant Mindset of the Bible.*

Simply put, *our Christian unity finds its roots in our participation in the new covenant.* I am not suggesting that we try to create a humanistic kind of unity, but that we seek to honor and preserve the sacred bond that God has *already* established through the new covenant in Jesus Christ.

Once again, we can glean much from one of Paul's letters to a local congregation:

> Therefore I, the prisoner of the Lord, implore you to walk in a manner worthy of the calling with which you have been called, with all humility and gentleness, with patience, showing tolerance for one another in love, being diligent to preserve the unity of the Spirit in the bond of peace. There is one body and one Spirit, just as also you were called in one hope of your calling; one Lord, one faith, one baptism, one God and Father of all who is over all and through all and in all. Ephesians 4:1–6

The spirit of this passage echoes that of Philippians 2:1–4. God calls His people to *diligently preserve* the unity of the Spirit by walking humbly, gently, and patiently, showing genuine consideration for other believers.

What Paul does not present in this passage, however, is a picture of uniformity. Uniformity demands that we all look the same, mimic each other's practices, and hold to identical doctrines. Such a mindset calls us to conform to human standards to gain acceptance.

I once dealt with a Christian organization that routinely criticized anyone outside its own theological system of belief. The leaders did not demand that their people isolate from other believers, but they did not need to. Plenty of social pressure was applied. Feigning concern for the "sheep," key spokesmen so often proclaimed the shortcomings of other ministry organizations that the people feared building relationships outside their sphere. This approach created an unhealthy dynamic in which everyone copied a small handful of leaders. Considerable pain and regret followed.

THE BODY OF CHRIST

The Creator of our vast cosmos is not the God of a mere handful. He is the God of a *multitude*—people of all races and nationalities, with a wide variety of distinctives and cultural practices. Some of us can accept this diversity, but only as long as "those" people stay "over there" and never enter the doors of our church. Christianity might work this way in our minds, but the Lord honors all His children with *equal* passion.

I have participated in worship gatherings with believers from around the globe, and the experiences were rich with God's presence. But as glorious as they were, those meetings provided but a taste of what heaven will be like:

> After these things I looked, and behold, a great multitude which no one could count, from every nation and all tribes and peoples and tongues, standing before the throne and before the Lamb, clothed in white robes, and palm branches were in their hands; and they cry out with a loud voice, saying,
>
> "Salvation to our God who sits on the throne, and to the Lamb." Revelation 7:9–10

Our Lord has *one* body, and that body is diverse. Moreover, because no group is superior to another, we can celebrate Christian diversity without envy, conceit, or judgment.

We have already highlighted statements by Paul in his letters to the Ephesian and Philippian churches. As yet another example, let us consider what he wrote to the Colossians:

> So, as those who have been chosen of God, holy and beloved, put on a heart of compassion, kindness,

humility, gentleness and patience; bearing with one another, and forgiving each other, whoever has a complaint against anyone; just as the Lord forgave you, so also should you. Beyond all these things put on love, which is the perfect bond of unity. Let the peace of Christ rule in your hearts, to which indeed you were called in one body; and be thankful. Colossians 3:12–15

Do you see a pattern? Once again, the esteemed apostle appeals for unity, and once again, he emphasizes the *attitudes* of believers toward one another. Thus, we can define Christian unity as *a relational oneness that is established through the new covenant in Christ and preserved through humble and practical love.* Such a love-based unity reveals God's glory and provides evidence of our relationship with the Creator of all things.

Churches need not consolidate into a single organization to be unified. We are free to worship with different styles, maintain different organizational distinctives, and even vary in doctrine regarding nonessential matters. We are not held together by conforming to a uniform norm. Instead, we preserve our bond of unity as the new covenant family of God through sincere and humble love. *The church of God is bound together by covenantal love, not by sameness.*

Theologically, I would be labeled a Pentecostal. I suppose that in itself creates a barrier for some Christians. But ever since that prayer experience when the Lord "adjusted" my kingdom perspective, I have not hesitated to cross denominational boundaries. I have prayed and worshiped often with brothers and sisters from diverse streams and have spoken extensively in traditional churches. Were all those spheres vibrant and healthy? By no means. Did I agree with every jot and tittle of their theology? Not at all. But in each sphere, I found people who genuinely loved the Lord, and the new covenant became the primary bond that allowed us to move beyond denominational labels.

Too often, we make the mistake of confusing *culture* and *command*. For example, worship is a Biblical command, but the modes and methods are free to change. Robes, hymnals, and liturgies; screens, pianos, and guitars—all are merely tools to aid in the worship of our glorious King. *What matters most is not the mode or method, but glorifying God through hearts of selfless love.*

How we worship is *cultural*; it changes with time and geography. A worship service in the first-century church would vary greatly from a worship service in Victorian England, which would look very different from a modern worship service in Peru.

To love one another is a *command* central to the New Testament. How we err when we exalt our cultural traditions over the Biblical command to honor and esteem one another in love! And what tragedy unfolds when the people of God lose sight of their purpose to bring light into this world as they dishonor other believers who differ.

Uniformity forces people to conform to a norm and creates division in the long run. *Unity binds us together and can endure the rigors of time because its roots stem from the free expression of love that characterizes Christian living.*

I hope we never forget the universal truth that unity strengthens and division weakens. Perhaps that is why the apostle Paul put it so well in saying, "Beyond all these things put on love, which is the perfect bond of unity" (Colossians 3:14).

REFLECTION

1. How might the covenantal mindset of the Bible differ from our understanding of relationships today?

2. According to Ephesians 4:1–6 and Colossians 3:12–15, what are some characteristics of the attitude Christians should hold toward one another?

3. How do unity and uniformity differ as they relate to freedom?

CHAPTER FOUR
TRUE GLORY

—◆—

But God has so composed the body, giving more abundant honor to that member which lacked, so that there may be no division in the body, but that the members may have the same care for one another.

1 Corinthians 12:24b–25

The deepest longing for the human heart is to know and enjoy the glory of God. We were made for this.

—John Piper

When we consider what separates Christians, we often think of differences in theology, religious practice, and lifestyle. This perspective is entirely natural, but those things need not separate us. Rather, it is *pride* that rises like a mountain to create our biggest obstacle to unity.

Debi and I have been married for almost forty years. And though we both grew up in small Western Pennsylvania towns, we are different in many ways. She is female; I am male. That difference alone involves multiple facets. My wife grew up in a loving middle-class family and attended church weekly. I grew up poor in a broken family. I do not remember my father ever attending church; my mother did so nominally. Debi studied accounting; I studied chemistry. Both are somewhat geeky, I admit. Still, they are worlds apart. Debi is consistent and easygoing (mostly), not very complicated, and generally content. Much of my life has been defined by struggle, and I am never satisfied to hover around the surface issues of life.

Debi and I have not had many serious conflicts throughout our four decades of married life, but when division tries to take root, pride is always the obstacle that keeps us at a distance. Whether it comes in the form of selfishness, stubbornness, or a sense of self-importance, pride—not our differences—has always posed the greatest threat to our relationship.

GLORY AND UNITY

The call to unity is a call to *humility*. But the humble path of God does not travel in a direction many people expect. Let us consider, once again, Jesus' High Priestly Prayer:

> "The glory which You have given Me I have given to them, that they may be one, just as We are one; I in them and You in Me, that they may be perfected in unity, so that the world may know that You sent Me, and loved them, even as You have loved Me." John 17:22–23

Embedded within this passage, we find a fascinating statement: "The glory which You have given Me I have given to them, that they may be one, just as We are one."

What was Jesus saying? What does glory have to do with unity? To make sense of His words, we must go back—way back—to the garden of Eden.

When God created humans, He made them *in His image* (Genesis 1:27). What an amazing honor to be created in the likeness of the King of Glory! The Bible does not say this about any other created beings—not the angels or the cherubim or the seraphim—only humans.

At the end of Genesis 2, we then read a seemingly innocent statement:

And the man and his wife were both naked and were
not ashamed. Genesis 2:25

They were naked and unashamed. No fear of vulnerability or
exploitation tormented the hearts of Adam and Eve. But as they
nibbled on the forbidden fruit, a seismic shift began. Suddenly,
they felt naked and tried to cover themselves with fig leaves. What
changed? Why did they now feel exposed and vulnerable?

GLORY DEFICIENT

Before they ate from the tree of the knowledge of good and evil,
Adam and Eve walked in intimate fellowship with God and were
clothed in His resplendent *glory*. But trusting the serpent over the
Lord, they went rogue and chose a path of independence. That
singular choice separated our first parents from their Creator and
from the "clothing" of His glory. Having been created for glory, its
sudden loss jolted them into an awareness never imagined. They
then reached for the fragile leaves of a fig tree in a vain attempt to
cover their shame. Apart from Jesus, each of their descendants has
followed suit.

Every human is born *glory deficient*. So, not long after birth,
we set out on a "glory quest." We labor hard, searching for approval
and success—all in an effort to establish a sense of significance
within ourselves. And though many of us experience moments
of glory-induced euphoria, our innate need to feel special and
important can never be satisfied apart from God. Human glory
rises and falls, but always fades in the end. Satisfaction lasts for but
a moment, and we are ever starved for more.

People no longer dress themselves with literal fig leaves, of
course. But we do use other means such as *appearance, performance,
possessions, status, knowledge,* and *association with others* in
our never-ending quest to establish a positive sense of identity.
Suspicious of the frailty of these "fig leaves," we then wrestle with
fears of vulnerability and exposure.

The pursuit of human glory—we might call it "imitation-glory"—creates a wedge between people even on the same team. Issues such as envy, judgmentalism, and elitism all find their roots here. Essentially, we are vying against each other for "god status"—an honor that can be attained only by One. Consider this a universal truth: human flesh boasts—or wants to boast—in itself.

Our innate glory deficiency compels us to seek goodness within ourselves, which is why judgmental attitudes ever plague our social spheres. How natural it is to look down with disdain upon those who fail to meet our standards. We live beyond a mere awareness of others' shortcomings, though, and often focus on all that is wrong. Such irony! Where would we be if the Lord held us to the same kinds of standards we impose upon others?

The pursuit of imitation-glory divides us, and for unity to be realized, our glory deficiencies must be satisfied. This need can never be met by natural means. Being a member of the oldest church in town or the fastest-growing denomination will do nothing to bring favor with God. Worse still, boasting in earthly status assails the throne of heaven. We need a better way!

Our glory deficiencies can be met only by looking to the Lord to lift us from the muck of spiritual infamy.

And you were dead in your trespasses and sins, in which you formerly walked according to the course of this world, according to the prince of the power of the air, of the spirit that is now working in the sons of disobedience. Among them we too all formerly lived in the lusts of our flesh, indulging the desires of the flesh and of the mind, and were by nature children of wrath, even as the rest. But God, being rich in mercy, because of His great love with which He loved us, even when we were dead in our transgressions, made us alive together with Christ (by grace you have been saved), and raised us up with Him, and seated us with Him in the heavenly places in Christ Jesus, so that in the ages to come He might show the surpassing riches of His grace in kindness toward us in Christ Jesus. For by grace you have been saved through faith; and that not of yourselves, it is the gift of God; not as a result of works, so that no one may boast. Ephesians 2:1–9

How amazing that the King of Glory would honor us as beloved *sons* and *daughters* in His family! Paul wisely adds verses eight and nine to remind us that we can do nothing to deserve such a lofty status. *Our Lord's grace enables us to experience the euphoria of heavenly glory without being corrupted by the pride that so often destroys human relationships.*

Glory is a special honor from God that brings the weight of true greatness to our lives. And according to Jesus, we can be one in Spirit because He shares His glory with us. When Christians begin to see themselves as equals, causes for division vaporize. The very idea is simple yet profound—especially in an age when celebrity mindsets have infiltrated even the church.

But can it be true? Does the King of Glory really want to extend such honor to us—sinners who were once His enemies? Without question! In the Old Testament, when God said He would not share His glory with another, He was speaking in the context of idolatry (Isaiah 42:8). Never will the Lord share His glory with a false god. *But God does want to share His glory with the children He so dearly loves!* No, we cannot reach out and grab glory by self-effort, but we can receive it as a gift of grace.

The Almighty God has lifted us from the cesspool of sin and exalted us to sit with the dignitaries of heaven. As Christians, we are now privileged and honored members of heaven's Royal Family. This means that none of us is more exalted than another. And if no one is superior, neither is anyone inferior.

DIVIDED BY LAW

Returning to Paul's letter to the Ephesians, we read:

> For He Himself is our peace, who made both groups into one and broke down the barrier of the dividing wall, by abolishing in His flesh the enmity, which is the Law of commandments contained in ordinances, so that in Himself He might make the two into one new man, thus establishing peace, and might reconcile them both in one body to God through the cross, by it having put to death the enmity. Ephesians 2:14–16

Paul was writing to a group of *Gentile* believers—people who were despised by the self-righteous Jews of His day. Those Jews felt superior—spiritually elite, if you will—because they obeyed the Mosaic law and lived up to heaven's standards of righteousness. Or so they thought.

The context of Ephesians 2:14–16 addresses the division created by self-righteousness in relationship to the Mosaic law, but a broader principle also applies. Our cultures are full of religious, moral, and social law codes. Some are written; many are not. The people who attain to the standards of those codes are deemed to be "righteous," while those who fail are seen as unrighteous and inglorious. Functioning within such a paradigm creates hostility, fuels conflict, and separates us from one another.

Self-righteousness of heart is often revealed by the words we speak about others—including our brothers and sisters in Christ. By giving attention to what we say about other people, we can get a pretty good idea of where our source of righteousness lies. And, to put it bluntly, the simple act of looking down upon another person with conceit reveals an incomplete grasp of the gospel on our part.

UNITED BY THE CROSS

Through the cross of Jesus Christ, every standard of religious, moral, and social righteousness comes crashing to the ground. No one is deemed worthy of glory within his or herself. No one. Our only source of real glory comes through the shame of the cross. Through faith in Jesus, we are all put on equal footing. If no one is superior, and no one is inferior, enmity cannot take root.

As we begin to understand these concepts, we realize that jealousy has no place in the body of Christ. Neither is there room for envy, or for having an attitude that despises another believer. The Lord gives equal honor to all Christians, and He desires to bless all equally.

There is a glory far greater than growing a large church, having the best worship service, or holding to "perfect" doctrine. It is found through humbly and selflessly loving our brothers and sisters in Christ. As we love one another with pure hearts, God's glory is revealed and His kingdom expanded in the midst of humanity.

Christians are not competitors vying to be "king of the hill," or striving to get the most people to a meeting. Darkness flourishes through such base thinking. Instead, we are *co-laborers* for the gospel. You play your part, and I play mine, but we all work together for the cause of Christ. If we can embed this one simple truth in our thinking—that we are co-laborers and not competitors—it will unleash the power of the church in amazing ways. And how our communities will benefit!

The idea of equal glory might sound noble, but in practice, it offends our pride. We naturally want to see ourselves as superior to others and much prefer to earn our sense of significance rather than receive it as a gift of grace. Unity is elusive because it comes at a steep cost to the human ego. As A. W. Tozer wisely stated, "The glory of God always comes at the sacrifice of self."

The Christian gospel is not just a call to salvation from our sins, although it certainly is that. The gospel is also a call to a *grace identity*. No longer do we labor like the world, trying to eke out a sense of significance through productivity and success. Instead, our identity is firmly established as the covenant children of God, and it is this honored status as sons and daughters that enables us to love freely, selflessly, and humbly.

Our world suffers through endless conflicts because people perceive identity through a natural, material lens. But being in Christ means that fleshly identities fade into the background. We do not dismiss our physical differences; we proclaim that our significance is found through Jesus and not human flesh. Only as we grasp our royal status as the children of God can we honor the diverse members of His body with genuine love.

Until we understand that the good news of salvation and the security of our identity in Christ form a single message, we will continue to clash with one another. But if we can get it, if we can grasp the essential dynamics of our royal status in heaven's family, our lives, our churches, and our communities will be forever changed.

I understand this perspective of glory is uncommon in many church circles.[1] Perhaps that is why we have been so divided. But not only is God's plan for shared glory mostly overlooked, it is also powerful beyond comprehension!

REFLECTION

1. What do you think our relationships would be like if pride were not a factor?

2. How does the pursuit of glory divide us?

3. How does the cross of Christ unite us?

---

1. Those who want to explore the issues of glory and identity more thoroughly can do so by reading my forty-day devotional, *From Glory to Glory: Finding Real Significance in an Image-Driven World.*

CHAPTER FIVE

FORGIVENESS IS PERSONAL

❖

So, as those who have been chosen of God, holy and beloved, put on a heart of compassion, kindness, humility, gentleness and patience; bearing with one another, and forgiving each other, whoever has a complaint against anyone; just as the Lord forgave you, so also should you.

Colossians 3:12–13

To forgive is to set a prisoner free and discover that the prisoner was you.

—Lewis B. Smedes

Many years ago, after a dynamic leadership meeting, I engaged in a personal conversation with a ministry friend. We discussed some amazing similarities between our life experiences, which helped our conversation go deeper. But as he talked, I became more and more concerned. Even though my friend was an active leader in Christian ministry, he held strong feelings of bitterness toward a man who once hurt him deeply. That bitter root had then snaked its way into his current ministry relationships. And the more my friend talked, the darker his mood grew.

I tried to be as understanding as possible. I had been betrayed myself and knew well the pain involved. I also realized that many of the man's complaints had just cause; several of his observations were well founded. Even so, I had a difficult time reconciling his bitter state with the teachings of our Lord and Savior, so I felt compelled to address the issue.

Graciously but firmly, I challenged my friend. "I can relate to your pain, but you cannot serve as a Christian leader while allowing such darkness to hold sway over your heart." Sadly, my words fell on deaf ears. He would not forgive, no matter what the Bible teaches. Nor was he open to talking through the issues with a mature leader or trusted counselor. The conversation ended, and I walked away brokenhearted over his stubbornness.

Not long after, due to seemingly unrelated circumstances, he was removed from his leadership position. He then lost his ministry altogether. Then, tragically, he lost his beautiful family due to divorce. Today, I do not even know if he is walking with the Lord.

We dare never forget that forces of spiritual darkness ever seek to deceive and destroy. We clutch bitterness tightly to our chests because of anger toward others, but the ill intent always boomerangs. We suffer. Our families suffer. Our friends suffer. Just about everyone we care about suffers when we refuse to let go and forgive. Forgiveness is personal, but it affects so many other people.

HARDNESS BLINDS

As Christians, we rarely give sufficient attention to the dangers of a hardened heart. In many ways, a hardened heart is like having cataracts. The cornea of the eye becomes thicker and calloused. Vision dims, colors fade, and clarity is lost. But it all happens so subtly that the person can remain unaware for a very long time.

Matthew 24:12 tells us that as lawlessness increases, human love grows cold. There are plenty of reasons to become cold and hardened in our fallen world; people can be so mean and selfish! And the harder we become, the less we see with our spiritual eyes.

Perhaps we were offended or betrayed. Or maybe a business or government entity stole our resources. It could be that somebody treated a loved one unjustly. The reasons might number in the millions, but the outcome is always the same: as our hearts become hard, our spiritual eyesight fails.

Few things can blind us more than a bitter heart that narrows our vision and darkens our perspective. In the end, all we see is the wrong done by others. And much of the time, we assume that heaven sees through our same dim eyes.

CHRIST'S TEACHINGS

In no way am I trying to minimize a person's pain or take lightly an injustice. But I cannot reconcile professing to love God with ignoring His command to forgive. The causes of a bitter heart can be very real, but how we respond is a matter of life and death. That is why Jesus spoke so strongly about the matter.

> "Be on your guard! If your brother sins, rebuke him; and if he repents, forgive him. And if he sins against you seven times a day, and returns to you seven times, saying, 'I repent,' forgive him." The apostles said to the Lord, "Increase our faith!" Luke 17:3–5

Jesus' command to forgive without merit is so extreme that it took even His disciples off guard. Furthermore, when they asked the Lord to teach them how to pray, part of that prayer included, "And forgive us our debts, as we also have forgiven our debtors (Matthew 6:12). Then, just to ensure that the message was clear, He added a necessary reason to let go of bitterness:

> "For if you forgive others for their transgressions, your heavenly Father will also forgive you. But if you do not forgive others, then your Father will not forgive your transgressions." Matthew 6:14–15

The teachings of our God leave *no* room for compromise—no matter how we try to justify our refusal to forgive. God's deep love will not allow darkness to thrive in the hearts of His own.

But Jesus did not just preach forgiveness; He also practiced forgiveness. In the most extreme circumstances, when bitter thoughts could have flooded His mind, our Savior cried out to His heavenly Father asking forgiveness *for those who were crucifying Him* (Luke 23:34). Love was more than a teaching that fell from Jesus' lips; it was a virtue that characterized His heart. For the Son of God who proclaimed Himself to be the Son of Man, forgiveness was personal.

FROM THE HEART

I once heard a woman speak about a painful experience she was working through. She said something like, "I have to forgive him because I'm a Christian, and the Bible says I won't be forgiven if I don't." I am not making light of her pain, but that woman missed the point of it all.

If we understood the full measure of our sins and the damage they have done, we would know that our transgressions against God far outweigh any offenses against us (see Matthew 18:21–35). And that is saying a lot because some of us have experienced terrible things at the hands of others. But the Lord understands our pain and has even entered into it through the cross. *We can forgive because He has forgiven even our worst offenses.*

The process of releasing an offense might vary, depending on the severity of your situation. Most often, forgiving involves making a *conscious choice*. If the pain runs deep, I suggest making a *verbal proclamation* of forgiveness using the person's name and addressing the specific offense. "Dear God, I forgive _____ for doing _____ to me. Please grant me the grace to do this from my heart." Tears might flow, and your prayer might be halting, but it is always to your benefit. Taking that first step was quite painful for me, but forgiving has become much easier since.

You might also consider recording your proclamation in a private journal, along with the date. If dark and bitter thoughts begin to creep back into your mind—as they likely will—you can pull out your journal and stand on the truth of what you have done. It might require a few reminders, but the declaration you made with your mouth will eventually make its way into your heart. In other words, your feelings will follow your actions.

If the injustice done against you created intense trauma, forgiving might involve more of a process. A friend of mine was once raped by a knife-wielding assailant. She and her husband knew they should forgive, but their hearts overflowed with anger toward the man who violated her. And so, they asked for prayer. And they consulted with wise leaders. And they met with a counselor. And somewhere in that process, they forgave. Today, my friend is emotionally whole and suffers no anguish when talking about that experience. If you cannot bring yourself to forgive in this instant, you can at least take steps to get help and move toward forgiveness.

REVEALING GOD'S GLORY

I do not know what pain you have experienced, but I do know forgiveness is always personal because pain is always personal— especially when we have been hurt by other Christians. And it matters not whether the offense was deliberate or unintentional. Nor does it make a difference if the person is apologetic or stubborn. We forgive because we know it is the right, best, and God-honoring action to take.

Forgiving, we should know, does not require forgetting. Nor is it the same as trusting another person. We are simply choosing to let go of a personal offense. I can forgive an accountant who stole my money, but that does not mean I will allow him near my finances in the future. Forgiveness can be immediate, but trust must be earned through the passage of time.

Regardless of how the process looks, forgiving an offense reveals God's glory. In doing so, it sends a powerful statement to demonic forces, declaring that light triumphs over darkness.

Forgiving an offense also strikes a powerful blow against evil's ability to torment. Bitterness is a trap laid by the enemy of our souls. No person who is unwilling to let go of a bitter past can move forward toward a hope-filled future. To forgive is to take a powerful step toward freedom. *We do not lose when we forgive. Instead, we triumph over evil.*

If we do not forgive, not only will we be overcome by evil, we will also open the door for evil to overcome those we love. But when we forgive, we crush the powers of darkness under our feet. The Lord of Light always wants what is best for us, and that means forgiving those who have done us wrong. Only then can we be truly free from the dark shadows that would envelop our souls.

Unity becomes possible only as we learn to "breathe" forgiveness because, trust me, we will experience many offenses as we relate to other Christians. Imperfect people will never be perfect in their behavior. This is our reality, and we are all guilty of shortcomings and offenses.

I wish I could say that every situation will end with a happy reconciliation, but such is not always the case. People will not always respond as you want, but forgiving can set *you* free from a dungeon of festering pain.

You might need to talk through an issue with someone. Or maybe you just need to hold your tongue when lashing out seems justified. But no matter how the surrounding circumstances look, you always need to forgive. If you cannot do it for the person who hurt you, or for yourself, or for your loved ones, forgive to honor the Savior who has forgiven you at a steep price through the cross.

REFLECTION

1. Read Ephesians 4:17–24. What does this passage speak to you?

2. In what ways does bitterness hurt the person holding onto it?

3. Is there someone you need to forgive? What steps can you take in that direction?

CHAPTER SIX

NAVIGATING DOCTRINAL DIFFERENCES

---◆---

This is His commandment, that we believe in the name of His Son Jesus Christ, and love one another, just as He commanded us. The one who keeps His commandments abides in Him, and He in him.

1 John 3:23–24a

Some believe they're God's German Shepherds whose purpose is to bark at others as they protect Him and His Word from evil doers.

—John Stanko

Doctrinal differences present us with one of the most significant challenges to Christian unity. Far too often throughout the centuries, arguments over doctrine have marred our human expression of the Christian faith. A multitude of church splits have followed. But should this be?

Should faithfulness to the Word of God require distancing ourselves from other devoted servants of Christ? Not necessarily. But to navigate this challenging issue effectively, we must first establish our *common ground*. Common ground is where we meet, and we must determine whether it is sufficient for us to be unified.

As our local pastors' network began to develop, we felt the need to adopt a basic *statement of faith*. That statement read as follows:

- We believe the Bible (Scripture) to be the inspired and only infallible, authoritative Word of God. (2 Timothy 3:16–17)

- We believe in the Trinity as eternally existent in three persons: Father, Son, and Holy Spirit. (2 Corinthians 13:14)

- We believe in the deity of Jesus Christ, His virgin birth and sinless life, His miracles, His vicarious death and atonement through His shed Blood, His bodily resurrection, and His ascension to the right hand of the Father as both the High Priest and sacrificial Lamb of God. (1 Corinthians 15:3–5— see also Luke 1:26–35; Acts 10:38; Romans 3:25–26; 1 Timothy 3:16; and Hebrews 1:1–8, 4:15)

- We believe that for the salvation of lost and sinful man, self-effort is futile and, thus, cleansing by the blood of Christ and regeneration by the Holy Spirit are essential. (Acts 4:12; Ephesians 1:7–8a, 2:8–9; and Titus 3:4–7)

This brief doctrinal statement established our common ground and became foundational to our group's existence; we even printed it on our brochure. If a new pastor expressed interest in joining, that individual knew immediately where we stood regarding the central tenets of the Christian faith. These truths, in our hearts and minds, were *nonnegotiable*. We determined that our unity would be in Christ alone, and refused to sacrifice our devotion to God to get along. Indeed, it is our devotion to the Lord that binds us together.

COVENANT ESSENTIALS

An old adage, often attributed to Augustine, says, "In essentials unity, in nonessentials liberty, in all things charity." This statement reflects well the heart of Christian unity. We cannot compromise essential doctrines. Historically, believers have suffered horrible persecution rather than deny the deity of Christ or the purity of His gospel of grace. If we fail to hold to the essentials, our "version" of Christianity becomes yet another in a long line of humanistic endeavors established on a false foundation of natural wisdom.

There are many other doctrines of the Christian faith that we can esteem as important but not necessarily essential. In Acts 15, we read of a sharp disagreement between the people of God that took place over the Mosaic law, and specifically, the rite of circumcision as related to salvation. The issue was deemed to be so significant that Paul and Barnabas, along with some others, were sent to Jerusalem to inquire of the apostles and elders.

If ever Christian leaders sought an opportunity to hand down a list of rules or doctrinal qualifications, that was it. If ever there was a time to create a comprehensive document stating the desirable and undesirable actions for Christian living, that was it. But the early church fathers did something different. Wisely, they addressed only the essentials—those issues worthy of separation.

The nature of the concerns highlighted in Acts 15 warrants our attention. They were *covenant related*, involving faithfulness to a new covenant relationship with God and preserving the sanctity of the marriage covenant. Never did the council propose a "believe what you will" mentality. *The early church found its unity by calling for faithfulness to God's enduring covenants.* May we do the same!

We cannot sacrifice truth for the sake of unity, but neither should we destroy the unity of Christ's body in the name of truth. All too often, it is our pride that separates us more than our theological perspectives. We become convinced that our doctrine is superior and that those who fail to embrace its wisdom are somehow lacking in their faith—or maybe even standing against "God's beacon of truth" (i.e., us). This mindset creates problems.

RIGHTEOUSNESS BY FAITH ALONE

None of us has perfect doctrine. Because we were born into sin, we all hold biases that taint our ability to see clearly. Only Jesus, the Son of Man, lived unaffected by self-centered motivations. He alone possessed a crystal clear understanding of truth.

"I can do nothing on My own initiative. As I hear, I judge; and My judgment is just, because I do not seek My own will, but the will of Him who sent Me." John 5:30

Who can say that he or she is perfectly yielded to God's will *all* the time? What one of us can claim perfect insight into the unseen spiritual world? The apostle Paul wrote that "we have the mind of Christ" through the presence of the Holy Spirit (1 Corinthians 2:16), but there is a *plurality* to his statement. Yes, we have the source of all truth dwelling within us, but only *collectively* can we discern the whole of that truth.

Think back, for a minute, to your earlier beliefs—the ones you proclaimed when your youthful wisdom reigned superior to the gray-haired souls whom you saw as clueless in life and doctrine. Have any of those beliefs changed throughout the years? Most likely. Why? Your ideas were confronted by reality, challenged by others, and illuminated by the Holy Spirit. Through the work of the Spirit, combined with the wisdom of other believers, you came to realize that your vision was limited. Such a process, we must realize, is *ongoing* in all our lives.

Yes, God can give us a solid handle on the essential doctrines of the faith, but that does not mean we understand everything. Nor does His blessing on our lives and ministries indicate doctrinal perfection. *The Lord blesses His children through covenant faith, not because we are perfect in doctrine and religious practice.* Believers who are devoted and blessed can still embrace some false doctrines and utilize unhealthy practices.

The pursuit of truth stands central to Christian living; we dare not treat it lightly. Still, doctrine often divides us because of a grave mistake in our thinking. Righteousness comes *only* through faith in Jesus Christ. But when *perfect doctrine*—as defined by our own organizations—becomes our *standard for righteousness*, we enter the narrow world of legalism in which judgmental attitudes thrive.

Without the dynamics of faith and love functioning as they should, truth can easily become our standard for righteousness. And when our supposed righteousness comes through knowledge of truth rather than through the cross of Christ, we create a web of conceit, judging all who fall short of our standards. As much as Christians preach grace, we seem hesitant to offer it to our brothers and sisters with different theological perspectives.

Do we love truth? Yes! Do we seek truth? Yes! Do we proclaim truth? Yes! Do we stand for truth? Absolutely! I am a teacher of God's Word, and accurately unpacking eternal truth always holds a central place in my efforts. But righteousness comes through faith alone, and we teach doctrine so God's people can abide in His love.

THE GOAL OF OUR INSTRUCTION

Sound doctrine provides the foundation for healthy Christian relationships, and those relationships should lead to honest and open dialogue. If we routinely become offended or upset when discussing doctrinal issues, something is off-kilter.

How ironic that the pursuit of accurate doctrine so often separates us when the opposite should be true! Paul reminded the young pastor Timothy that "the goal of our instruction is love from a pure heart and a good conscience and a sincere faith" (1 Timothy 1:5). If our doctrine does not lead us to a greater love for our brothers and sisters, something is off.

The apostle John also wrote that "if we walk in the Light as He Himself is in the Light, we have fellowship with one another" (1 John 1:7). Can another believer really be at fault when I am the one holding judgment in my heart?

I am not saying that love triumphs over truth, but that truth leads us to love. Truth matters. Our religion is called "Christianity," not "loveianity." It is all about knowing Christ and doing His will, and His will is for us to walk in *both* truth *and* love.

The pursuit of truth should lead to a "divine convergence" of sorts. I am not referring to a New Age philosophy, but rather to simple geometry. If you are pursuing truth with your whole heart and I am pursuing truth with my whole heart, we should be converging in the same general direction. If not, something is off.

Having been given a stewardship by God, I esteem sound and accurate doctrine more than most people. I work hard to make sure I get it right. I pray, and I read, and I study. And what a delight it is when I meet someone whose beliefs and practices mirror mine. We both have been pursuing truth, and that pursuit is converging around the reality of God. But there are other times when I meet a devoted believer with a different perspective or emphasis. And though I might not come to embrace that perspective fully, I am often enriched by it.

You seek after truth wholeheartedly, and I seek after truth wholeheartedly. You believe in salvation by grace through faith in the sacrificial death and resurrection of Jesus Christ. I do, too. I will meet you, then, in Christian brotherhood before the throne of God.

In that day, we will see clearly that His favor is not limited to those who worship like us and share every point of doctrine. Nor will we see denominational neighborhoods in heaven. We will not walk along Baptist Boulevard or recline in the lush green grass of Methodist Mall. We were all born with sinful tendencies and all became enemies of God. Only through the cross do we find righteousness and acceptance before God. Let us wholeheartedly pursue truth with humble hearts that converge at the cross.

In this life, agreeing perfectly on everything will be a rarity; different people will always have varied perspectives. In my wife's eyes, a sink garbage disposal is a near-necessary convenience. To me, a garbage disposal is a clogged drain waiting to happen. Unless she becomes a plumber, I do not think we will ever agree entirely on the matter. But that does not make us love one another any less. At least, I hope not! And, thankfully, there is so much more that we do agree upon. Even though my wife Debi and I differ on some issues, we are still of one heart and united before God in covenant.

SYSTEMS OF BELIEF

I once attended a presentation hosted by a church that had lost its theological bearings. When responding to questions, the speaker repeatedly referred to the doctrines of their denomination as established by its founder. I could not help but ask, "What are you following, the teachings of a man or the teachings of the Bible?"

We commonly divide God's family by elevating systems of belief and theological schools of thought above the unbiased pursuit of Biblical truth. This approach often involves trying to pull verses out of context so they can conform to our belief systems. That is not how God intended life to work. Biblical truth should form us, not the other way around.

We can argue about God's sovereignty as opposed to human free will, for example, but we find verses in the Bible that support *both* perspectives. Such tension between poles is reasonable in principle, but our analytic minds often find it unacceptable.

I sometimes wonder how committed we are to open and honest dialogue—especially in light of the loud, intimidating voices in our movements. Are we digging deeper into the Scriptures with honest hearts, or are we simply repeating what we have been taught? Are we fully yielding to God's truth, or are we afraid of being ostracized if we fail to follow the common path accepted within our movement?

ADJUSTING OUR ATTITUDES

Those who cannot easily refute a person's beliefs often resort to assaulting that individual's character. Declaring others to be "apostates" or "false prophets" makes it easier for us to discard their perspectives. After all, if they are not true believers, uniting with them would amount to yoking ourselves with darkness.

How do we respond when someone rejects Christianity because of the hypocrisy of professing Christians? We point them toward Jesus and Biblical truth. Along the same lines, what gives us grounds to invalidate a certain belief even if the person holding that belief is flawed? Are we ourselves without shortcomings?

Some doctrines are worth arguing over, and I have had those arguments. But when I encounter someone with beliefs I recognize to be false, I must take care to search my heart to ensure that it is free of judgment or bias. Only then am I in a position to establish a healthy dialogue. That dialogue must also involve asking clarifying questions so I can fully comprehend what is being taught. Sadly, I have seen well-meaning Christians publicly attack pastors for beliefs they never even held.

We begin by seeking to understand, and as we understand, our perspectives might shift. Or perhaps, we will better grasp the nature of an error and be better positioned to humbly explain how a doctrine deviates from truth.

The love of God does not belittle or cut off another person for seeing a different perspective of truth. Love endeavors to search out truth and bridge the gaps that separate us. But if our supposed esteem of Biblical doctrine leads us to conceit, judgment, or condemnation, something is off. Our attitudes can miss the mark even when we have the issues right.

Regardless of the source, division makes the church irrelevant in a society, and when the church loses influence, even the craziest ideas will flourish. May we represent our Lord well by treating one another with honor and working out our differences respectfully!

REFLECTION

1. What makes it necessary to have a firmly established set of doctrinal beliefs?

2. What are the evidences of sound doctrine?

3. What is the value of open and honest dialogue when our beliefs differ?

CHAPTER SEVEN
FACTIONS

————————◆————————

The one who says that he is in the Light and yet hates his brother or sister is in the darkness until now. The one who loves his brother and sister remains in the Light, and there is nothing in him to cause stumbling. But the one who hates his brother or sister is in the darkness and walks in the darkness, and does not know where he is going because the darkness has blinded his eyes.

1 John 2:9–11 (NASB)

I have never yet known the Spirit of God to work where the Lord's people were divided.

—Dwight L. Moody

Tens of thousands of Christian-related "denominations" populate our world. I have seen estimates as high as 45,000 or more. Many of these organizations were formed as the result of a God-given vision, but many were not. How do we make sense of so much division in a belief system that is supposed to be unified by love?

Sometimes love compels us to separate ourselves. History reveals a multitude of church splinters and splits. Some of those divisions were not only justified, they were necessary. When Christian organizations abandon the core elements of our faith, or when they corrupt the teachings and practices of Scripture, separation might be the only God-honoring solution.

The apostle Paul addressed the issue of factions in his correspondence with the church in Corinth:

> Now I exhort you, brethren, by the name of our Lord Jesus Christ, that you all agree and that there be no divisions among you, but that you be made complete in the same mind and in the same judgment. For I have been informed concerning you, my brethren, by Chloe's people, that there are quarrels among you. Now I mean this, that each one of you is saying, "I am of Paul," and "I of Apollos," and "I of Cephas," and "I of Christ." 1 Corinthians 1:10–12

In context, the divisions Paul criticized were identity (glory) based. Reading the entire letter, it appears that many in the Corinthian church struggled with insecurity as a result of being social outcasts. In search of a meaningful identity, they aligned themselves with esteemed leaders so they could share their perceived glory. Because these immature believers were living by natural wisdom, the church experienced division even in its early days.

SOME DIVISIONS ARE NECESSARY

Later, Paul changed his tone. Factions were necessary, he said, to show those who were "approved" (1 Corinthians 11:19). What did he mean? Because of its grace-rich message, the Christian faith casts a wide net. People with all kinds of backgrounds, motives, and desires are invited into God's fold. But not everyone drawn to the Christian message responds in a way that honors God (for example, Acts 8:9–24 tells the sad story of Simon the Sorcerer). This is especially true in our modern era. Covenantal thinking has been lost, and the gospel is often presented merely as a "choice," without reference to repentance, surrender, or water baptism.

Regardless of our shortcomings, the freedom inherent to Christianity and the message of salvation by grace allow for false believers. As long as the church exists on this imperfect planet, there will be fraudsters, hypocrites, and false prophets—or whatever else you want to call them. In His wisdom, the Lord will tolerate false believers for a season, as He taught in the parable of the wheat and tares (Matthew 13:24–30). Thus, we will have factions within and between church organizations.

The reality of false believers reminds us of the importance of establishing essential doctrines. Certain issues, such as the authority of the Bible, the deity of Christ, and the necessity of the cross are nonnegotiable. We will not compromise these for anything, nor does the Lord expect us to. But be advised, the message of forgiveness through the blood of Jesus alone is one that offends worldly sensibilities.

The pursuit of truth, we must accept, divides people. Our Lord Himself said, "Do not think that I came to bring peace on the earth; I did not come to bring peace, but a sword" (Matthew 10:34). Was Jesus contradicting the message of Christian unity? Not at all. The unity lauded by Scripture is a *covenantal unity* to be celebrated among those who are true believers. But with those who refuse to embrace the authority of God's Word and the exclusivity of Christ as the only Way of salvation, Christians will have conflict. Like it or not, such is our reality.

If holding true to faith in Christ means being ostracized or persecuted, then so be it. While God calls us to love and honor all people, we will honor no one above our Lord and Savior. He alone is the King of kings and Lord of lords, and Him alone will we worship. Like the faithful saints before us, we refuse to compromise the essential truths of God's Word for any reason.

We must ask ourselves, however, what role *we* as individuals play in the separation process. Are we inherently *peacemakers*, or are we ourselves the sources of unnecessary division? When I was a young believer, a wise pastor once said, "There will always be walls between you and some other Christians. Just be sure that you're not the one building them." What sage advice!

ENLARGING OUR VISION

How do we reconcile our fractured human reality with the Biblical emphasis on unity? *We choose to walk in humble love.* Christians often mistakenly believe that they alone are the faithful servants of God. Is this not what Elijah did when he despaired in the wilderness? "I alone am left" (1 Kings 19:10). But the Lord corrected the prophet's small-minded perspective: "Yet I will leave 7,000 in Israel, all the knees that have not bowed to Baal and every mouth that has not kissed him" (1 Kings 19:18).

Just because we hold true to the Word, and just because He moves in our midst does not mean that we alone are the true people of God. Such "us versus them" thinking is certain to splinter the body of Christ. Some of this divisive mentality comes from taking the Scriptures out of context.

> They are from the world; therefore they speak as from the world, and the world listens to them. We are from God; he who knows God listens to us; he who is not from God does not listen to us. By this we know the spirit of truth and the spirit of error. 1 John 4:5–6

In saying, "We are from God," the apostle John was referring to the *apostolic church*—of which he was a leader. The broader, universal application proclaims that worldly-minded people will not regard the true teachings of Christ.

Some leaders wrongly assume that only a select few represent the "we" in this passage. After all, if we adhere to the teachings of the Bible, and God answers our prayers, surely *we* are the "we" of 1 John 4:6. Therefore, anyone who refuses to accept our theological perspective must be of the world and caught up in a spirit of error.

I once experienced a confusing scenario created by this faulty mindset. Some members of our community had spearheaded an inspiring "March for Jesus" rally. Hundreds of believers gathered not to protest, but to sing and pray and celebrate God's goodness.

As we marched through town enjoying the fellowship of Christians from an array of churches, a group from an independent church began handing out tracts and shouting for us to repent because we had dared to welcome Catholics. A very strange scene that was! And if we felt it odd, I cannot imagine what unbelievers thought.

The idea that we alone are the true church and all others are apostate or fraudulent proclaims a lie. In these last days, our Lord is raising up a vast and diverse body of believers. Any one organization forms but a part of a greater whole. To think otherwise is to fall into the trap of self-conceit that doomed ancient Israel.

Perhaps we should echo King David's soul-searching prayer:

> Search me, O God, and know my heart;
> Try me and know my anxious thoughts;
> And see if there be any hurtful way in me,
> And lead me in the everlasting way.
> Psalm 139:23–24

Self-conceit reflects one of the most dangerous and insidious forms of pride because of its deceptive nature. Only by dealing honestly with the state of our own hearts can we address the issue of Christian unity in a way that glorifies our Lord. *The true church of God is not recognized by its aloofness but by its extreme love for the entire body of Christ.*

THE MARK OF SOUND DOCTRINE

As important as the essential doctrines of our faith might be, Christians also champion many beliefs and practices that are not essential. Therefore, building close relationships with those who hold differing doctrinal perspectives need not be considered a dangerous compromise of our faith.

Glory is found not in having "perfect" doctrine. Rather, sound doctrine will produce the fruit of humble love, and it is in the realm of love that a greater glory is manifested. When we reach across the aisle to love and honor a fellow believer (who holds a different opinion), the Lord takes delight and manifests His glory.

We can make a similar argument regarding race. The United States has seen considerable division between blacks and whites throughout the years. Those divisions have even spread to Christian churches. What a tragedy! When we focus on the attributes of the flesh and honor the opinions of humans over the sacred bond of the new covenant, we stray far from the dynamics of vibrant Christian living. Many then suffer. *Sound doctrine tells us that the mark of sound doctrine is love for our brothers and sisters in Christ, regardless of race.*

Those who choose to honor the unity of the faith will most certainly experience times of frustration and disappointment. It is part of the nature of working with people—even true believers. So what should we do? Persevere in love! I am not suggesting that we turn a blind eye to bad doctrine or injustice, but that we deal with issues humbly and graciously. Love is the mark of Christ's disciples because only by grace can we love as He loves.

REACHING OUT

I mentioned in Chapter One how the Lord blessed our efforts working with campus ministers at our local university. However, I did not include the many frustrations and disappointments we experienced along the way. When a new campus minister came to the university, I would often buy the person lunch, provide insights about the campus, and offer my availability, if needed. Over time, those efforts helped create a culture of Christian oneness. Not everyone, however, responded as I had hoped.

I remember having at least three difficult conversations with campus ministers I had previously welcomed to the university. Men of God were not behaving as men of God should. I do not see myself as one of God's "correction police," but each of those circumstances required speaking the truth in love to provide some necessary correction.

Their reactions to my efforts were mixed. One individual admitted that his behavior with a young woman was out of line, and he chose to move in the direction of repentance. The others continued in their obstinate ways. In the end, our fellowship was severed because they refused to admit their transgressions and submit to the authority of Scripture.

Would it have been better to ignore those men when they first came to the university? No. That would be like closing our church doors to visitors because of potential problems. During those years, I also welcomed several others who proved to be godly, devoted, and faithful laborers for the gospel. The value of those relationships far exceeded any problems created by the few.

In an ideal world, all who profess Christ—and especially all who serve Him on a vocational basis—would want to conform their lives to His desires. But as previously stated, we do not live in an ideal world. Factions will develop. Even so, another person's lack of love does not excuse our own.

WALKING IN THE LIGHT

Is it possible to contend for truth and also walk in love toward a brother or sister with whom we disagree? Certainly. The two are not mutually exclusive. Yes, we are stewards of the mysteries of God and must contend for the integrity of the gospel. But it is here that the *state of our hearts* means everything. That is a primary—if not *the* primary—issue in the eyes of our heavenly Father.

Our brothers and sisters in Christ need not be perfect in every practice and belief—certainly we ourselves are not—for us to love and honor them. They need only be covenant members of the family of God. Other issues can be worked out as we seek to preserve our covenantal bond in Christ. But even if we never come to see eye to eye, we can still have fellowship—as long as we all choose to walk in the light of God's love.

Light attracts light. If Christians repel one another, we must ask if someone has given darkness a foothold.

This is the message we have heard from Him and announce to you, that God is Light, and in Him there is no darkness at all. If we say that we have fellowship with Him and yet walk in the darkness, we lie and do not practice the truth; but if we walk in the Light as He Himself is in the Light, we have fellowship with one another, and the blood of Jesus His Son cleanses us from all sin. 1 John 1:5–7

One of the key thoughts in John's letter involves the state of a believer's heart. *If we fail to walk in love, we walk in darkness.* This stark truth compels us to ask questions—especially if we have disassociated ourselves from other Christians. But what questions are we asking? Are we honestly examining our hearts and motives to see if we are walking in the light of God's love? Or are we looking for reasons to distance ourselves from those with whom we disagree? Are we trying to "de-Christianize" other believers to excuse our own lack of love?

Disagreements will occur among people who are passionate for God and His mission. Think about the conflict between Paul and Barnabas over John Mark that occurred before their second missionary journey (Acts 15:36–40). Paul's later references to the two men imply reconciliation. It might have taken a little cooling-off time, but they eventually worked through their issues.

I also find it interesting that their disagreement took place sometime around AD 48–50—before Paul penned his passionate pleas for unity in the body of Christ. That firebrand of an evangelist never wavered in his devotion to the gospel, but he also seemed to value Christian oneness more as he became seasoned in life and ministry.

Life on earth is messy, and we are all self-willed, imperfect people. Conflicts will be inevitable. But if the Lord calls us to love even our enemies, how much more should we genuinely love our covenant brothers and sisters in Christ? If we cannot honor the family of God, are we truly abiding in His love?

GOD'S KINGDOM FIRST

Many Christians in our modern era have made the mistake of adopting political methods and strategies in their quest to positively influence the government. The concept of being in the world but not of the world certainly applies here.

That we would want to influence political decision making is both understandable and necessary. Government leaders affect so much. However, the world of politics is a nasty one, generally characterized by divisive strategies such as manipulating opinions and belittling opponents. Belittling reflects conceit, and conceit reveals an incomplete grasp of the gospel of grace.

The political realm builds its kingdoms upon foundations of simmering rage. Most people, I have found, care little about the government as long as their needs are met apart from intrusive policies. So, to stir the public to action, party leaders will stoke the fires of fear and rage. Media outlets add fuel to the flame because rage generates mouse clicks, which in turn generate dollars. Meanwhile, the soul of the nation rots. Just because we are not bitter does not mean we are not hardened.

Truth and justice do not depend upon our political affiliation, but we try to make it that way. I routinely see Christians magnify the wrongs of candidates in opposing parties, while justifying the wrongs of those they favor. How can heaven be pleased? So called "truth" that is driven by personal bias is nothing more than personal opinion—even when couched in noble language.

Sadly, many Christians have bought into divisive and unjust mindsets while seeking favorable political outcomes. But as *ambassadors for Christ* (2 Corinthians 5:20), where does our primary allegiance lie? Is it to a national government? To a political party? To a certain candidate? Or is our primary allegiance to the kingdom of God?

Heaven's kingdom is of a far higher order than any human government, and its mindset differs vastly from that of the political realm. The arguments from the political right and left might differ, but ironically, both are often characterized by the same biased, critical spirit. When we raise our noses in self-conceit, in many ways we disqualify ourselves as effective witnesses for God's kingdom.

How is it that some Christians can treat those across the political aisle as despised Gentiles? Are these the type of factions that honor the Lord and advance His purposes? When employing fleshly attitudes and methods to bring change, we might win a few battles, but we will alienate hearts in the process. In this, we must thoughtfully weigh our goals. Is an effective witness for the gospel our primary concern? Or are we elevating issues that might be important but not essential?

We must also choose our battles carefully. Some issues are worth contending for. Others are not. Those who fight unnecessary battles will lose their focus, strength, and credibility for the ones that matter most.

Collectively, we are fighting an intense, life-and-death war for the soul of our nation. How we treat one another matters because this conflict takes place in the realms of faith, love, and prayer.

When we belittle and criticize other believers, we help fulfill the devil's divisive plans. And if the children of God cannot triumph over the darkness that would separate us, no one can. If we cannot work through our personal offenses to genuinely love one another, no one can. It might seem impossible at times, but humble, persistent love will always triumph in the end!

REFLECTION

1. In what types of situations are factions necessary?

2. What makes self-conceit so dangerous?

3. Please read 1 John 1:5–7. What does it mean to "walk in the light," and how does doing so influence our relationships with other members of God's covenant family?

CHAPTER EIGHT
RESOLVING CONFLICT

——————◆——————

If possible, so far as it depends on you, be at peace with all men.

Romans 12:18

Conflict is inevitable, but combat is optional.

—Max Lucado

During my college ministry years, I once drove to the Pittsburgh airport with a group of Chinese students to help pick up their arriving spouses. Afterward, we stopped by an ethnic Chinese store for them to buy groceries. One of their preferred desserts was ice cream, and the flavors of choice were *green bean* and *red bean*. In all my days, I had never thought of associating a vegetable with ice cream.

If we had a mind to, we could try a wide variety of unusual flavors worldwide. Jellyfish (it glows in the dark), raw horse flesh, mushy peas and fish, (venomous) mamushi snake, duck liver, and mint leaves with sea urchin meringues would all be options. That people would even try some of these flavors is beyond me, and it says much about our potential for conflict.

The Lord created people to be diverse, and the differences reveal His handiwork. But when we add self-centeredness, self-will, and self-glorification to the mix, conflict becomes a part of daily life on this planet. How ironic in a world that craves intimate relationships!

If we want to see the beauty and experience the fulfillment of unity, we must develop a vital skill: *the ability to resolve conflict well.* Sadly, conflict resolution is becoming a rare art in our day. And if we are not taught such skills by our parents, broken relationships will multiply with each passing generation. Thankfully, these are skills we can each develop, even though the learning process will at times be painful. As my friend Todd likes to say, "We have two primary options: avoid uncomfortable situations, or seize them as opportunities for growth."

As much as I wish every problem could be addressed through prayer alone, there are some issues that require physical action on our part. Moreover, writing this book would be much easier if I simply appealed to our desire for relational oneness, but I feel the need to include some basic principles of conflict resolution. The ideas need not be complicated, but neither are they easy to implement because people are diverse, imperfect, and prideful.

TEN STEPS

The following ten steps do not provide a comprehensive plan that promises to resolve every conflict to your complete satisfaction. Still, they can help you develop interpersonal skills so that close, meaningful relationships become more than a faraway dream.

1. **Seek to understand our heavenly Father's perspective.** We all tend to make life about us, but our part in this universe is quite small. It is our Creator's perspective that matters most, and getting His vantage point is one of the best ways to begin resolving a conflict. The Bible tells us that God is not partial (Romans 2:11), and that righteousness and justice form the foundation of His throne (Psalm 89:14). In other words, He is like an *objective* parent who can discern a situation without the emotional biases that so often cloud our judgment. "Lord, please open my eyes to Your perspective," is a great prayer to help begin the process.

However, seeking to see our relational situations through God's eyes does not have to wait until we are in the middle of a conflict. I highly recommend reading through the book of Proverbs from time to time. Within its thirty-one chapters, we find precious nuggets of wisdom that will help both avoid and resolve conflict.

2. Honor the covenants. Covenant relationships are sacred in heaven's eyes, so we should treat them with reverence as well. Too often, though, we do the opposite. Why do we so often treat worst those whom we should treat best? Is it because we are familiar with them? Ungrateful? Hurting?

Seeking to honor a covenant relationship does not mean becoming a "doormat" for others to tread all over. Rather, as we work out our issues, we seek to glorify the Lord by honoring the sacred bonds He so highly esteems.

3. Search your heart and contemplate your motives. Reflection is a powerful tool for conflict resolution, but I am not referring to our common habit of continually replaying a scenario in our minds. We naturally want to extend blame, but an objective look at the motives behind our emotions can go a long way toward peacefully resolving a situation. "Why was I offended?" "Why am I angry?" "What is hindering me from wanting reconciliation?" All are questions we can ask ourselves when a relationship is strained. Taking such a step might prove invaluable at a time when we feel tempted to send off an angry message full of regrettable words.

4. Choose to forgive. Our ability to forgive does not depend upon full reconciliation of a situation. Instead, by choosing to forgive early in the process, we can set the stage for a faster, more complete resolution to the problem. And by choosing to soften our heart, we might lessen the risk of having it broken.

The act of forgiving can be momentarily painful. That does not make it bad, however. I would much prefer to see a person shed tears of pain through the process of forgiving than become calloused and hardened by refusing to forgive.

5. Put out fires while they are small. In dry times, even a small spark can create a massive blaze. The Ranch Fire, which combined with another to form one of the largest in California history, was reportedly started from a spark created by hammering a metal stake into the ground.

If you want to avoid unnecessary drama and exhausting conflicts, do not ignore problems with the hope that they will simply disappear. Instead, deal with issues while they are still small and before they get out of control.

Something similar applies to stopping the flow of gossip, which often fuels the fires of conflict. Try asking yourself some questions before sharing a sensitive matter with another person. Have I spoken with the offending individual first? Will this conversation bring healing or further division? Am I looking for a solution or just someone to agree with me?

6. Invite God into the situation through prayer. In so many ways, praying involves yielding control to the Lord. He always knows what is best, and He alone has the power to resolve seemingly impossible situations. Giving up what we want sets the stage for Him to do what He wants, which is always good.

Through prayer, we can also silence the demonic voices that delight in causing confusion, conflict, and division. Finally, prayer affords us a powerful opportunity to cry out to God for wisdom. He can teach us redemptive ways to handle conflicts that might have never entered into our minds otherwise.

7. Choose an effective method of communication, and use it. One drawback of modern technology is that it gives us the ability to communicate easily through impersonal means. Attempting to resolve a conflict by texting, for example, can spare us some uncomfortable moments, but much is lost since we are unable to observe body language or hear a tone of voice. These limitations might actually further misunderstanding and conflict rather than help resolve a situation.

If emotions are especially heated, or the potential for violence exists, we of course want to take special care. Writing a letter might be a less-than-perfect solution, but it also affords the opportunity to weigh our words before saying something we might later regret.

Sometimes, when tensions are running high, we might also consider involving an objective third party. Such a person would need to be mature, unbiased, and willing to risk the ire of the conflicted parties.

8. Seek to understand the other person's perspective. When we are wounded or angry, all we usually see is our own viewpoint. That can change as we ask nonthreatening questions instead of lashing out with accusations. In doing so, we want to avoid the types of questions that might make a person defensive, such as, "Why did you ignore me when I walked in the room?" A better approach would be, "I felt ignored when I walked in the room. Is there a problem between us, or was it just my imagination at work?" When we make a genuine effort to understand another person's viewpoint, we open the door for discussion and might be surprised by what we discover. We might also spare ourselves the humiliation of making a false accusation.

9. Speak graciously. Proverbs 15:1 tells us, "A gentle answer turns away wrath, but a harsh word stirs up anger." How difficult it is to resolve conflict when we strive to prove ourselves right or put another person in his or her place!

I know a man who once reached out to a Christian brother with whom he had a strained relationship because that was what he was "supposed to do." Unfortunately, his calloused attitude only complicated the matter.

We live our faith from the inside out. When angry or hurting, we want to enlarge our perspective and calm our emotions before speaking the truth in love. And if reconciliation is our goal, speaking harshly will only work against us.

10. Follow through. If you make a promise or commitment, do what you said you would do. Also, refuse to allow bitterness back into your heart. In an ideal world, we would always be happy with the outcome of a reconciliation effort. Reality, however, often differs. You cannot control another person's attitudes, words, or actions. But as long as you honor the Lord by doing your best to resolve the conflict, you can be at peace.

These steps should prove helpful, but conflict resolution can never be limited to a formula. God has given us each a free will, and people can be unpredictable. Dealing with others, especially in conflict, propels us into uncharted waters where we are not in control. We can, however, develop skills that help resolve conflict, while welcoming the kingdom of heaven to earth. Again, the process might not be easy or comfortable, but it is so very good!

REFLECTION

1. What are the drawbacks of always avoiding uncomfortable conversations?

2. Why is it vital to examine our own hearts before attempting to resolve a conflict?

3. What are the advantages of working to resolve a conflict in person rather than through digital communication?

Chapter Nine

False Prophets

◆

Now I urge you, brothers and sisters, keep your eye on those who cause dissensions and hindrances contrary to the teaching which you learned, and turn away from them.

Romans 16:17 (NASB)

Whatever disunites man from God, also disunites man from man.

—Edmund Burke

As if we have not dealt with enough challenging issues in this short book, let us now move on to the topic of false prophets. In no way am I naive to think that everyone who professes Christ seeks to truly honor Christ. Both Jesus and Paul warned about the danger of false prophets, and the latter did so with great emotion (Matthew 7:15–20; Acts 20:17–31). This is a serious issue that we dare not ignore, but it also requires a depth of wisdom that flows only from heaven's throne.

WHAT IS A FALSE PROPHET?

From a New Testament perspective, a false prophet professes to speak for God (the "God" might be himself), but consistently lives according to the fallen nature (flesh). Regardless of spoken professions, a false prophet will be self-centered, controlling, and self-exalting. These are the basic traits of human narcissism that frequently give way to greed and sexual exploitation.

False prophets often portray an image of false humility. They might profess to be humble servants of God, but the end goal is always self. And if the message of a prophet, teacher, or leader—or anyone, for that matter—proclaims the ability to attain divine status, you can be sure the deceptive hiss of the serpent is whispering in someone's ear.

During His sermon on the mount, Jesus provided some keys to identifying false prophets:

> "Beware of false prophets, who come to you in sheep's clothing but inwardly are ravenous wolves. You will recognize them by their fruits. Are grapes gathered from thornbushes, or figs from thistles? So, every healthy tree bears good fruit, but the diseased tree bears bad fruit. A healthy tree cannot bear bad fruit, nor can a diseased tree bear good fruit. Every tree that does not bear good fruit is cut down and thrown into the fire. Thus you will recognize them by their fruits.

> "Not everyone who says to me, 'Lord, Lord,' will enter the kingdom of heaven, but the one who does the will of my Father who is in heaven. On that day many will say to me, 'Lord, Lord, did we not prophesy in your name, and cast out demons in your name, and do many mighty works in your name?' And then will I declare to them, 'I never knew you; depart from me, you workers of lawlessness.'" Matthew 7:15–23 (ESV)

The context of this passage emphasizes the importance of the human heart. Our Lord was not railing against those who embrace the miraculous for today; He was using contrast to make a vital point. We identify true servants of God neither by gifts nor power (so often indicators of God at work), but by good *spiritual fruit*.

What do we mean by "spiritual fruit"? The Bible provides us with an understanding:

> But the fruit of the Spirit is love, joy, peace, patience, kindness, goodness, faithfulness, gentleness, self-control; against such things there is no law. Galatians 5:22–23

Spiritual gifts (*charismata*) are "grace gifts." Unmerited by the recipient, they do not depend upon a person's spiritual maturity, and do not indicate favored spiritual status. Nor are they given to fuel selfish purposes, but to more effectively love and serve others (1 Corinthians 12:7). In contrast, *spiritual fruit is the by-product of an abiding relationship with the Lord.*

> "I [Jesus] am the true vine, and My Father is the vinedresser. Every branch in Me that does not bear fruit, He takes away; and every branch that bears fruit, He prunes it so that it may bear more fruit. You are already clean because of the word which I have spoken to you. Abide in Me, and I in you. As the branch cannot bear fruit of itself unless it abides in the vine, so neither can you unless you abide in Me. I am the vine, you are the branches; he who abides in Me and I in him, he bears much fruit, for apart from Me you can do nothing. If anyone does not abide in Me, he is thrown away as a branch and dries up; and they gather them, and cast them into the fire and they are burned. If you abide in Me, and My words abide in you, ask whatever you wish, and it will be done for you. My Father is glorified by this, that you bear much fruit, and so prove to be My disciples." John 15:1–8

Mysteriously, spiritual powers can sometimes be accessed by ungodly people. But spiritual fruit is *relational*—the by-product of an intimate relationship with God. Fruit is also something that grows over time as a person matures in Christ.

When we walk with the Lord and abide in His presence, our character is transformed—not in an instant, but incrementally. Bearing sweet and abundant fruit—the foremost of which is *selfless love*—requires that we day by day humble our hearts and align with our Creator's ways.

A false prophet misses God's heart and "feeds" off the sheep for personal gain, rather than selflessly serving. I am not referring to just the obvious vices of greed and sexual immorality, though. If we build our sense of importance by feeding on the approval of people, we are identifying with false prophets more than with Jesus. Insecurity will lead us down a path of disobedience and deception as it turns even good intentions into toxic spirituality.

A friend of mine once became the leader of the men's group in his church. His efforts were effective, and the group began to grow. One day, the pastor wanted to talk. "I'm shutting down the men's group," he said. "It is becoming more popular than I am, and I can't have that in this church." The church was not a cult, and I would not necessarily call that man a false prophet, but he was certainly moving in that direction on a dangerous road of self-conceit.

The result of a self-centered, controlling, and self-exalting life is always deception. Sometimes, that deception is intentional; false teachings are knowingly used to dominate and control people. Other times, a false prophet is merely deluded, though the outcomes are no less devastating.

Self-absorbed leaders cast a dark shadow over what should be the most life-giving entity (the church) this world will ever know. The end result is that lost people will remain lost, while wounded sheep will likely depart from the Christian fold. A true tragedy.

SOBERING WORDS AND NECESSARY TRUTHS

Ignoring Christ's message of self-denial creates a deceptive environment that easily gives rise to false prophets.

And He was saying to them all, "If anyone wishes to come after Me, he must deny himself, and take up his cross daily and follow Me. For whoever wishes to save his life will lose it, but whoever loses his life for My sake, he is the one who will save it." Luke 9:23–24

Certainly, we want to celebrate our right-standing with God that comes through the cross of Jesus Christ. But if we do not also carry our own individual crosses of self-denial, our spiritual lives will produce the rotten fruit of sensual living. We are all born with wayward tendencies, and the false prophet within us must be crucified by denying selfish desires. There is no other way. God will not simply remove these cravings from us; we must nail them to our individual crosses (Romans 8:12–13; Galatians 5:16–24).

Those who preach faith, favor, and the blessings of God but fail to include a call to self-denial will create a dangerous and deceptive spiritual dynamic. For example, teaching about the blessings of prosperity but failing to caution impressionable listeners about the dangers of materialistic idolatry sets the stage for spiritual corruption to wreak havoc (1 Timothy 6:1–10).

Another grave theological error involves magnifying a cross of self-denial while minimizing the cross of Christ. In this case, personal sacrifice becomes a badge of self-righteousness. False prophets often use this approach to manipulate people into "obedience" and to fund their own selfish desires.

False beliefs breed not only bad teaching but also unhealthy actions. Dark ideas thrive in isolation, so false prophets will often disassociate from the greater body of Christ. Indeed, isolating people from family and friends can be a key identifier of a cult. But when we preach the truth of God's Word and walk in the light of His love, cult leaders tend to keep their distance, drawing near only in their attempts to gain influence or feed off "fresh prey."

That Christian leaders are wary of outsiders is often justified; they might simply be guarding the sheep that God has entrusted to them. But, alas, the apostle Paul reminds us that the problem of false prophets runs much deeper:

> Be on guard for yourselves and for all the flock, among which the Holy Spirit has made you overseers, to shepherd the church of God which He purchased with His own blood. I know that after my departure savage wolves will come in among you, not sparing the flock; and from among your own selves men will arise, speaking perverse things, to draw away the disciples after them. Therefore be on the alert, remembering that night and day for a period of three years I did not cease to admonish each one with tears. Acts 20:28–31

Paul's sobering words emphasize the life-and-death nature of Christian ministry. We cannot be naive about dark forces at work, even within the sphere of a local fellowship. Savage wolves exist, and if given free rein, will devour vulnerable sheep. All the more reason, then, that we be able to identify the signs of a false prophet.

WHAT TO DO?

Human relationships can be complicated, and that is especially true when dealing with those who appear to bear the fruits of a false prophet. How do we practically navigate this confusing issue?

When we began inviting local pastors to participate in our first community prayer initiative, I struggled with deciding whom to consider. Not all of them embraced Biblical Christianity. For that reason, I sent each one an advance copy of my *Community Prayer Devotional*. From the start, I wanted them to understand that we were established on the truth of God's Word. The approach worked well as we sought to celebrate a true unity in Christ.

I can say something similar about the wisdom of providing a basic statement of faith for our pastors' group. Our nonnegotiable doctrinal statement compelled others to make a choice. Not all

Christian pastors from the community joined our efforts, but neither did we get any that we considered to be false teachers.

The question goes deeper, however, than simply who attends a prayer gathering because false prophets have so much potential to damage and destroy human lives. I will often ask myself a series of questions when considering how to address the issue.

Do I have a relationship with this person? Is the individual negatively affecting those within my sphere of influence? Is this a person who is just beginning to stray from sound doctrine and practice, or someone who has been willfully living according to self? With only minimal effort, you might be able to win someone who strays momentarily. But positively influencing a person steeped in self-will and false teaching is far more difficult.

There are some nationally recognized teachers of the Bible that I simply choose to ignore. In many cases, their attitudes, words, or actions caution me to keep my distance. When I had my own "congregation" of college students, I dealt with negative influences from such teachers on a case-by-case basis—unless I became aware of widespread problems within our sphere. And if a leader from our local community concerned me, I was inclined to meet one-on-one to address my concerns.

I refuse to publicly belittle or demean those whose teachings I find problematic. If I feel the need is present, I will speak out, but there can be a vast gulf between addressing bad doctrine and verbally attacking a person. One grave danger we face with public criticism is that we bring judgment on ourselves when we verbally assail someone whom God favors. In particular, applying the label of "false prophet" to a spiritual leader is never to be done lightly.

How do we walk such a delicate line? How do we address significant errors in a way that honors God? It begins with remembering our Lord's passionate love for *all* His covenant children. In 1 Corinthians 11, just before Paul's teachings on spiritual gifts, we find a familiar passage that is both mysterious and challenging:

> For I received from the Lord that which I also delivered to you, that the Lord Jesus in the night in which He was betrayed took bread; and when He had given thanks, He broke it and said, "This is My body, which is for you; do this in remembrance of Me." In the same way He took the cup also after supper, saying, "This cup is the new covenant in My blood; do this, as often as you drink it, in remembrance of Me." For as often as you eat this bread and drink the cup, you proclaim the Lord's death until He comes.
>
> Therefore whoever eats the bread or drinks the cup of the Lord in an unworthy manner, shall be guilty of the body and the blood of the Lord. But a man must examine himself, and in so doing he is to eat of the bread and drink of the cup. For he who eats and drinks, eats and drinks judgment to himself if he does not judge the body rightly. 1 Corinthians 11:23–29

Some church leaders encourage congregants to "judge" themselves so they do not observe the Lord's Supper in an unworthy manner. In general, the admonition refers to lifestyle, but in context the apostle Paul was writing about how we relate to "the body." The big question is, what did he mean by failing to "judge the body rightly"? Did he have in mind the communion bread, or the body of Christ—as in the church?

I think both applications are warranted and intimately connected because both are covenant related. If a covenant is a sacred and binding relationship, it should never be treated as common. Thus, we should not approach the communion table casually because it represents a covenant meal. Nor dare we treat our covenant brothers and sisters in Christ with dishonor.

Remembering the larger context of 1 Corinthians 11:23–29, Paul brought up the topic of the Lord's Supper because he was addressing the relationships between Christians. That line of thinking runs both before and after his message regarding communion. And notice that Paul did not criticize the Corinthians for getting drunk (not that this was acceptable behavior). Instead, he focused on how they treated one other.

Removing the relational element from this passage misses God's heart and pushes the limits of accurate theology. When we partake of communion, we are proclaiming the Lord's death. Why did Jesus die? Our Lord paid the steepest of prices to deliver lost souls from the domain of darkness and elevate them as sons and daughters of His Royal Family.

When we gather to celebrate communion—how often that might be—we remember our Lord and His passions. And Jesus deeply desires both the well-being and the unity of His people. *To treat a beloved child of God with disdain is to despise the very covenant we profess to celebrate.*

These ideas echo words spoken by the Lord to the father of our faith. During the process of establishing a sacred covenant with Abraham (Abram), the Lord declared:

> "I will bless those who bless you, and him who dishonors you I will curse, and in you all the families of the earth shall be blessed." Genesis 12:3 (ESV)

This vital passage is steeped in covenantal thought. If someone would so much as dishonor Abraham (i.e., treat him lightly or with contempt), the Creator of all things would bind that person with a curse. Such a statement speaks volumes about how highly our Lord regards His covenant friends. But what, we must ask, happens when one of God's children maligns another? How do we reconcile such base behavior with the sacred nature of the new covenant that was initiated through our Savior's spilled blood?

Our flesh naturally wants to criticize and tear down others, so this question challenges us all. I recently watched a Christian brother perform a task poorly. It was not a situation that warranted correction, so I had only to make a simple choice: express my negative opinion or keep it to myself. I wanted to criticize, but as I weighed my thoughts, I realized they would serve no redemptive purposes. Was my goal to magnify the shortcomings of a brother in Christ, or did I want something better for him? Rather than helping anything, critical words would only tear down a faithful servant of God.

How many similar situations do we encounter daily? How often do we thoughtlessly criticize those our Lord regards as sons and daughters? How quick are we to demean the ones whom God elevates? I cannot help thinking that we take such behavior far too lightly. In so many ways, the loss of a sacred, covenantal mindset has done terrible damage to the church.

We might not normally connect Genesis 12:1–3 and 1 Corinthians 11:23–29, but both were penned with the sacred and binding nature of covenant relationships in mind. I cannot say I fully understand the consequences of treating another Christian with disdain, but I do have a healthy fear regarding the matter. Never do I want to be found violating a sacred covenant with my Lord by maligning a brother or sister who is near to His heart.

How we need both the wisdom and heart of our Lord as we navigate concerns about false prophets, false doctrine, and our treatment of other Christians! Love calls us to address such issues (and even the quality of work when appropriate), but doing so requires the wisdom of a sage. May we find grace to recognize and righteously address false faith, while also treating our fellow brothers and sisters as *co-heirs with Christ* who are honored and beloved in the eyes of our Father.

REFLECTION

1. What is a false prophet?

2. Why is good spiritual fruit needed in a leader's life?

3. Please read Genesis 12:3. What does this passage speak to you?

CHAPTER TEN
BRINGING CORRECTION

———◆———

All discipline for the moment seems not to be joyful,
but sorrowful; yet to those who have been trained by it,
afterwards it yields the peaceful fruit of righteousness.

Hebrews 12:11

Love precedes discipline.

—John Owen

In ancient cultures, kings were often *sovereign* rulers. Such men were not subject to democratic voting or the will of the people. Just or unjust, their words became the law of the land. To challenge a king's authority was to risk death. And so they committed cruelties of all kinds, with few apparent consequences.

The monarchy of ancient Israel differed—especially regarding consequences. Theirs was a nation created by God and established under His authority. When a king led his people into sin, the truly sovereign King would work to bring them back to their roots.

Israel's most highly regarded monarch, David, loved the Lord deeply, but his passions sometimes transgressed God-given boundaries. Such was the case when David impregnated the young woman Bathsheba and gave orders for her husband to be sent to his death on the front lines of battle (2 Samuel 11).

Risking his own life, the prophet Nathan obeyed God by confronting the king's sins. David admitted to his transgressions and humbled his heart in repentance.

THE BIG PICTURE

Because God gave us the gift of free will, and because we are prone to selfish living, and because we often lack wisdom, there will be times when correction is needed. No one is exempt. We live in an age of grace, but that does not give us license to do as we wish.

As with resolving conflict, bringing correction requires godly wisdom exercised with a humble attitude. Let us begin by considering a picture of healthy growth in Christ's church:

> And He gave some as apostles, and some as prophets, and some as evangelists, and some as pastors and teachers, for the equipping of the saints for the work of service, to the building up of the body of Christ; until we all attain to the unity of the faith, and of the knowledge of the Son of God, to a mature man, to the measure of the stature which belongs to the fullness of Christ. As a result, we are no longer to be children, tossed here and there by waves and carried about by every wind of doctrine, by the trickery of men, by craftiness in deceitful scheming; but speaking the truth in love, we are to grow up in all aspects into Him who is the head, even Christ, from whom the whole body, being fitted and held together by what every joint supplies, according to the proper working of each individual part, causes the growth of the body for the building up of itself in love. Ephesians 4:11–16

We are all in this together, and what happens among Christians matters. Our actions affect:

- Us as individuals
- Our children
- The people in the church
- Those outside the church
- The heart of our Lord and Savior

Growing together as the body of Christ sometimes requires us to have difficult, uncomfortable conversations. A mature brother or sister will seek to *speak the truth in love*, but what does that mean? The answer is simple enough. How would you want truth spoken to you? Would you want someone to come alongside as a friend to correct, strengthen, and encourage? Or would you prefer to have your face pushed into the dirt while onlookers gawk at the sight?

I have seen situations where church leaders failed to correct someone who was living sinfully. The resulting church decay negatively influenced both the members and the mission. And it affected not only the spiritually vulnerable, but also those more seasoned in the faith. Devoted Christians might have a heart to see lost and corrupt souls redeemed, but they do not want bad or immoral behavior within their church families.

FOR THE LOVE OF DISCIPLINE

Discipline, when given well and wisely, is one of the highest forms of love—although people do not always see it that way. No one wants to receive discipline because it feels bad. And through immature eyes, discipline not only feels bad, it also appears cruel.

When our children were young, they often expressed outrage at our efforts to correct them. But as parents, we understood that always allowing them to have their way would create massive problems in the future. Immature hearts and minds are selfish, and that leads to problems for everyone involved.

The book of Hebrews expresses well the importance of discipline:

> Consider him who endured from sinners such hostility against himself, so that you may not grow weary or fainthearted. In your struggle against sin you have not yet resisted to the point of shedding your blood. And have you forgotten the exhortation that addresses you as sons?

"My son, do not regard lightly the discipline of the Lord, nor be weary when reproved by him.
For the Lord disciplines the one he loves, and chastises every son whom he receives."

It is for discipline that you have to endure. God is treating you as sons. For what son is there whom his father does not discipline? If you are left without discipline, in which all have participated, then you are illegitimate children and not sons. Besides this, we have had earthly fathers who disciplined us and we respected them. Shall we not much more be subject to the Father of spirits and live? For they disciplined us for a short time as it seemed best to them, but he disciplines us for our good, that we may share his holiness. For the moment all discipline seems painful rather than pleasant, but later it yields the peaceful fruit of righteousness to those who have been trained by it.

Therefore lift your drooping hands and strengthen your weak knees, and make straight paths for your feet, so that what is lame may not be put out of joint but rather be healed. Hebrews 12:3–13 (ESV)

What powerful, unwelcome words! How we covet love but despise discipline! Yet it would be far worse for God to abandon us by allowing us to have our own way.

THE SPIRIT OF CHRISTIAN DISCIPLINE

Hebrews 12:3–13 speaks of the importance of discipline, but it also reminds us of *the spirit* with which we are to correct. *The goal of discipline is not to punish, but to form people into the image of Christ.* Healthy growth requires correction, and it is through such a lens that we should view discipline.

I have seen situations in which church leaders corrected too much, or corrected badly. Leaders are called to teach, exhort, and nurture their people, but they are not called to control their lives. We all struggle with imperfections; that is part of being human. Thankfully, the Lord does not overwhelm us by dealing with everything at once!

Handling a situation Biblically involves more than just our actions; attitudes matter, too. Some leaders will try to follow the letter of the New Testament but miss the spirit of it all. Absolutely, there is a place for identifying and challenging both false doctrine and bad behavior, but the attitude with which we do it means everything. The biggest problem I see with many corrective efforts is the harsh spirit in which they are made. As the people of God, we can do better by keeping redemption and restoration as primary goals.

RESTORING THE FALLEN

Jesus is the Savior of both victim and perpetrator. He never minimizes sin, but always seeks to redeem and restore *all* involved.

During my campus ministry years, several of our students began attending a church that seemed unhealthy. Not wanting to malign the authority of the pastor, I did my best to deal with the questionable teachings as they affected our group. But when the man developed an unhealthy (nonsexual) relationship with one of our former students, I knew it was time to meet with him.

Without question, this man had strayed from the truth and was entering false prophet territory. But though he had gotten turned around, he still loved the Lord in the depths of his heart. Even before our meeting, the pastor humbled himself by reaching out to another leader in our community for help. I am happy to say that because the man humbled himself, the Lord redeemed and restored the situation. Today, we call each other friends.

There have been several other times when I reached out to fallen brothers. Some humbled themselves and repented. Others did not. For those who genuinely loved the Lord, a gracious response to their failure meant everything. The bottom line is that we do not win hearts with condemnation, but with humble and gentle—brotherly, if you will—correction.

> Brethren, even if anyone is caught in any trespass, you who are spiritual, restore such a one in a spirit of gentleness; each one looking to yourself, so that you too will not be tempted. Galatians 6:1

Once again, we return to the theme of *humble love*. Yes, we are to protect the sheep and guard against false prophets. And yes, we should call to account those who stray onto the broad road of sin. But as it is with seeking to reconcile a broken relationship, our attitude can mark the difference between failure and success.

Let us strive to see people through our Savior's eyes. That means taking care to call out doctrinal error instead of verbally attacking an individual, and critiquing actions before applying labels. And let us never forget to guard our own hearts as we seek to guard and protect the sheep entrusted to us:

> Watch over your heart with all diligence,
> For from it flow the springs of life.
> Proverbs 4:23

Quite honestly, humility, kindness, and gentleness are the virtues I most often see lacking in the realm of public correction. Where is the fruit of the Spirit in our corrective efforts? Where is the patience? The kindness? The gentleness? Where is the desire to preserve the unity of the Spirit in the bond of peace?

When we treat fellow believers—or even unbelievers—with harsh and demeaning attitudes, what message do we send to a watching world? Do we reflect the heart and teachings of Christ, or do we mirror the Pharisees? I am not calling for compassion without truth, but rather truth steeped in compassion.

Neither do we want to humiliate people or their family members when we bring correction. We can help prevent such unnecessary trauma by continuing to remember that our goals are always to redeem and restore rather than punish.

CORRECTING WISELY

There is a time to discipline sternly, but that depends upon the response of the person being corrected. We should give special attention to a principle established by Jesus:

> "If your brother sins against you, go and tell him his fault, between you and him alone. If he listens to you, you have gained your brother. But if he does not listen, take one or two others along with you, that every charge may be established by the evidence of two or three witnesses. If he refuses to listen to them, tell it to the church. And if he refuses to listen even to the church, let him be to you as a Gentile and a tax collector." Matthew 18:15–17 (ESV)

The apostle Paul echoed Christ's instruction when he wrote, "Shall I come to you with a rod, or with love and a spirit of gentleness?" (1 Corinthians 4:21). The strength of our correction should depend upon the receiving person's response.

We always begin gently and privately, intending to challenge, restore, and encourage. But if the response is selfish or hardened, we might need to ramp up the intensity of our efforts—especially if other people will be adversely affected by wayward actions. In many ways, this was how God dealt with the nation of Israel.

> Do not harden your hearts as at Meribah,
> As on the day of Massah in the wilderness,
> "When your fathers put Me to the test,
> They tested Me, though they had seen My work.

> For forty years I was disgusted with that generation,
> And said they are a people who err in their heart,
> And they do not know My ways.
> Therefore I swore in My anger,
> They certainly shall not enter My rest."
> Psalm 95:8–11 (NASB)

The very last thing the Lord wanted was to deal harshly with the children of Israel; they pushed Him into it by their stubborn refusal to obey His ways. But when the people humbled themselves with repentant hearts, the Lord dealt gently.

At the beginning of this chapter, I mentioned King David's reprehensible behavior toward Bathsheba and her husband Uriah. Psalm 51 records David's brokenhearted response to the Lord's discipline. The king had transgressed the Mosaic law, but he also understood the spirit of divine discipline:

> The sacrifices of God are a broken spirit;
> A broken and a contrite heart, O God, You will not despise.
> Psalm 51:17

DEALING WITH CHURCH ABUSES

Some people believe they have been appointed by God to call out abuses within Christian organizations. As much as I wish it were otherwise, recent history has revealed the need for their voices to be heard. When a church, for example, protects abusers and callously ignores the pain of the abused, are not its leaders violating a sacred trust? These types of cancers have festered far too long, and if accountability is not going to come from within, it must come from somewhere.

Seeking to preserve the unity of the Spirit does not equal overlooking abuses, oppression, and injustice within Christian circles. If a church, ministry, or denomination refuses to protect its most vulnerable—for whom the Lord cares deeply—something is off. More often than not, seeking to "bury" an abusive situation indicates deep-rooted problems. Church leaders who are more concerned about image or money than the well-being of their people have lost their spiritual bearings.

Even attempting to protect the effectiveness of a ministry provides an insufficient excuse for failing to deal with an issue of abuse. If the situation is handled with integrity, the ministry will likely recover and possibly be more effective in the long run. But if it is handled poorly, the harm might be irreparable.

Ravi Zacharias led a large, powerful, and effective ministry for many years. But he also had a serious problem with how he treated women. People raised concerns about his behavior from time to time, but the leaders around him failed to address them adequately. In the end, both his reputation and the ministry they sought to protect suffered irreparable damage. Even worse, multiple women experienced the trauma of his abusive behavior.

Using Paul's admonition in 1 Corinthians 6 regarding lawsuits as their justification, some church leaders refuse to involve civil authorities in cases of abuse. All the while, they ignore the spirit of 1 Corinthians 5 by failing to call the perpetrator into full account for his actions.

If we were to weigh the gravity of sins, I would say that spousal abuse and sexual molestation are at least as reprehensible in the eyes of heaven as sleeping with a stepmother. How can we allow such actions to be taken without serious consequences? The fact that the New Testament does not mention a specific action does not make it unimportant. If we grasp the spirit and intent of a passage, we can wisely make application in other circumstances.

These types of situations can be especially complicated because victims of abuse must also process their pain and guard their hearts. We are not responsible for injustices done against us, but we are responsible for what we do with our pain. Raw emotions tend to cloud our vision. Truly seeking righteousness and justice requires that we process our pain at the foot of the cross so it comes out as love rather than as a bitter agenda. By all means, let us strive to protect vulnerable people and the integrity of the Christian faith. But may we never lose sight of the fact that we are each responsible for our own thoughts, words, and actions.

God's call to unity challenges us as we encounter false beliefs, false living, and false prophets. Regardless of the issue at hand, a necessary step involves searching our own hearts to ensure we are truly honoring our Lord. May God give us grace to stay true to Him by walking humbly and correcting gently whenever possible. And may we strive to protect those entrusted to us while doing everything within our power to preserve the unity of the Spirit in the bond of peace.

REFLECTION

1. Why is discipline necessary for healthy growth?

2. In what ways does discipline reflect love?

3. Please read Psalm 51. What can we learn about God's love and David's response to the prophet Nathan's correction?

CHAPTER ELEVEN

TEARING DOWN WALLS AND BUILDING TRUST

◆

So then we pursue the things which make for peace and the building up of one another.

Romans 14:19

Every cord that binds me to Christ also binds me to my brother, and I can't break one without breaking the other.

—E. Stanley Jones

I once spoke with a friend who expressed frustration over a disagreement with her husband regarding a theological issue. Here were two people, who had been happily married for well over a decade, debating about the teachings of the Bible. Their struggle is by no means unique. A wholehearted pursuit of truth will lead us in the same direction, but we will always have differences of perspective to navigate.

The apostles Paul and Barnabas disagreed sharply because of differing perspectives regarding John Mark (Acts 15:36–40). Paul the evangelist saw a weak-faith youngster who had abandoned the cause of the gospel when the mission started to get difficult. But Barnabas the encourager viewed John Mark as a young man who needed nurturing to reach his full potential.

On a less important level, my wife likes mustard; me, not so much. I am enamored by the beauty of nature; she would be fine with urban living. Debi places a high value on the care of our household; I can sometimes be a domestic moron. Our situation involves two people who grew up in small Western Pennsylvania towns and have been married for decades. How many more perspectives do we find in the body of Christ that includes a vast number of people from different racial, national, geographic, and economic backgrounds?

The diversity of Christ's body is why love, not uniformity, serves as the perfect bond of unity. Different people with differing backgrounds (and hormones) will always have differences. But if we are rooted in Christ, we can still be anchored to one another.

DANGEROUS TERRITORY

How we navigate our differences speaks volumes about our spiritual maturity, or lack thereof. I do not need to agree fully with a person's lifestyle and beliefs to love and accept that individual. I simply need to love. People who must have others see things their way often become argumentative and even divisive. And divisiveness, to be sure, is dangerous territory.

God views unity with such high regard that Paul instructed Titus to "reject a factious man after a first and second warning, knowing that such a man is perverted and is sinning, being self-condemned" (Titus 3:10–11). Divisive people tend to be hard-hearted and hold tightly to offenses. All too often, they focus on all that is wrong with someone else. Their callous disregard for Christ's body then creates problems of all kinds.

Though I preach the unity of the Christian faith, I do not get along with everyone. I am not beyond fault, but I try to be self-aware and search my heart when a conflict arises. Only rarely have I taken the painful step of dissociating from a person because reasonable dialogue became impossible. Sadly, some people see only their agendas, making honest discussions and meaningful relationships virtually impossible.

Honoring the unity of the faith is not easy; I will give you that. Intentional efforts to tear down walls and build trust are required.

Trust is sacred, and healthy relationships will never flourish apart from it.

In my work with pastors, I have found that disunity is often rooted in a lack of trust. The idea that pastors would not trust one another seems a bit strange. After all, Christianity is built upon love and faith. Even so, pastors commonly struggle with trusting others beyond their sphere. Sometimes they are merely protecting their flocks from potential false prophets. But all too often, a lack of trust is due to past betrayal, an experience with "stolen" sheep, or a territorial mindset.

A friend of mine serves as a chaplain in a mental health correctional facility. Because it is run by the state, chaplains from several denominations and religions work there. A resident once asked her for materials relating to a particular denomination. My friend had concerns about some of their doctrine, but still gave the young man materials produced by the denomination itself. She was excited to see him moving toward God and wanted to fan the flames of his faith. Sadly, the chaplain for that denomination exploded in anger and began berating my friend. How dare she give out materials that belonged to another organization! This type of "territorialism" not only reveals a feudalistic mindset, it also does terrible damage to pastoral relationships—not to mention the people they are professing to serve.

I knew of another pastor who committed a grave sin—more than once. Precious lives were damaged, and much pain resulted. When he again exhibited the actions of a wolf, several pastors in the community exhorted his church leaders to remove him from the pulpit and deal with the problem. Based on the number of hurting people who came to them for counseling, they felt he needed supervised time to deal with his issues before being restored to ministry. What was the response? "Yes, what he did was wrong, but we have forgiven him." The man was back in the pulpit a week later.

Those leaders were devoted to Christ, but they failed to understand that the pastor had betrayed a sacred trust. Certainly, forgiveness for sins can be immediate, but broken trust can be rebuilt only over time. Foundations of trust might crash to the ground in an instant, but the rebuilding process will always be tedious and time consuming. Their failure to understand this distinction meant he would likely commit the same transgression again. And he did—multiple times—until they had no choice but to remove him from the position entirely. In the meantime, he violated more people who then struggled to trust Christian leaders from any church, not just their own. Some, I can imagine, had trouble trusting even God.

A CRISIS OF TRUST

We live in an era when people are becoming less and less trusting of one another. I would even say we are facing a *crisis of trust*. Whether we speak of business, government, or church spheres, suspicion runs deep on almost every front. And for good reason! Suspicion, unfortunately, is normal and often warranted.

A recent move compelled me to navigate multiple real estate transactions. What made me most anxious in the process? I did not know whom to trust. One potential buyer made a generous offer on our building, but much about him seemed questionable—in spite of the fact that he invoked God's name. Sadly, I have seen more than one scam perpetrated by someone who professed the name of Jesus. These types of concerns are a reason why we produce detailed contracts. If we lived by a covenantal mindset, however, many of those contracts would be unnecessary.

In today's world, simply expecting Christians to have faith in one another is naive. Intentional efforts are necessary to tear down walls and build trust. Such intentionality plays out on both the micro and macro levels. Whether we speak of a small group of eight people, or relationships between pastors in a community, trust is rarely instantaneous. And when people do not have opportunities to meet regularly to get to know one another, establishing trust becomes all the more difficult.

BUILDING TRUST

Understanding the relational dynamics involved, several in our local pastors' group began taking steps to tear down walls and build trust with other churches and their leaders. One pastor began to pray the Lord's blessings upon other community churches during his Sunday morning services. There were no stealth criticisms or negative critiques, only prayers for the Lord's favor and blessing.

Another church used a community workday to bless some local fellowships. They contacted their pastors and asked about unmet needs around their properties. Church members then donned their work clothes and set out to paint and landscape as a gesture of good will. How delightful those results turned out to be!

Trust can also be built in other, more subtle ways. How a church welcomes new visitors can prove a powerful indicator of its kingdom perspective, or lack thereof. If a visitor comes from another church, a wise pastor will ask questions about why the individual left and if there are relationships that need to be healed. The idea is not to simply increase church attendance, but to make sure God's kingdom is being rightly advanced.

A kingdom-minded leader will also elevate a visitor's needs over personal desires. I know several pastors who commonly say, "I would love for you to attend here, but if you find that our church is not a good fit, I'll help you find one that is." Making such a statement presents a powerful way to build trust. Visitors recognize the pastor's genuine concern and often spread the word to friends and family.

One highlight of my experience with our local pastors' network took place when we invited pastors and their spouses to share an evening meal with their community colleagues. While volunteers cared for their children, the adults dined at tables of eight, sharing stories and getting to know one another. A bit of humorous entertainment followed. By the end of the evening, several couples were making plans to gather on their own. The transition from potential competitor to colleague to friend was at work. And upon that foundation of trust, the group was able to move forward in a dynamic way.

If we have a heart to, the Holy Spirit will reveal ways to bless Christians both within and outside our church walls. Any single step might not mean much, but we dare not underestimate the cumulative influence of incremental efforts to build trust.

The key idea in all of this is *intentional edification*. We either focus on building others up, or we fixate on how they fall short. Why should we always seek to edify other Christians? They are "living stones" in the glorious temple of God (1 Peter 2:4–5). What contractor tears down what he is trying to build? We are also members of the same body. When the parts of a body attack one another, we call that a painful "autoimmune disease."

Edification reflects the heart of God. *If we are truly holding fast to the head, which is Christ, we will seek to build up the body, which is His church.* Those who live with the mindset of edifying others will develop a reputation for being trustworthy. In time, this will give them a powerful voice to speak into human lives.

Rather than maintaining the all-too-common status quo of divided Christians fulfilling their own agendas, we must take intentional steps to tear down walls and build trust. We begin by laying our own hearts open before God. Then we work to reach out and bless others. The results might seem meager at first, and momentum might take time to build. But if we truly love the Lord and care about our communities, we will persist in navigating the challenges. In this way, His glory will be revealed for all to see.

REFLECTION

1. Give an example of a breakdown of trust in our culture.

2. Why is trust so easy to shatter and so difficult to rebuild?

3. What practical steps can you take to tear down walls and build trust with other Christians?

CHAPTER TWELVE
A BLESSING OF LIFE

—◆—

"For My house will be called a house of prayer for all
the peoples."

Isaiah 56:7b

Caesar hoped to reform men by changing institutions
and laws; Christ wished to remake institutions, and
lessen laws, by changing men.

—Will Durant

Turn on the news and you can be depressed in no time! It does not
matter if we speak of local, national, or international headlines;
on every level we hear of violence, abuse, and injustice. Living the
news is even worse. Whether it be a shooting across the street, a
domestic dispute next door, or a drug overdose in the bathroom of
the corner convenience store, pain and grief abound.

Some of the most heartbreaking stories involve neighborhood
violence—especially in areas where impoverished people have
no viable options for escape. Few scenes move the heart like a
devastated parent weeping over the loss of a beloved child through
senseless violence.

In places where violence and death are common, we often
hear local leaders and family members proclaim, "The violence
has to stop!" But it does not. No human has the power to demand
change into existence, no matter how deeply the desire might run
in our hearts.

The causes of violent crime are many, but that does not prevent us from identifying trends. Social issues such as sexual immorality, fatherlessness, poverty, racism, and injustice all combine to form a tangled web of human brokenness.

SPIRITUAL STRONGHOLDS

Behind all the visible factors that undermine our collective well-being, dark spiritual forces work to wreak havoc and destruction. All too often, though, we live blind to the spiritual realm.

> For our struggle is not against flesh and blood, but against the rulers, against the powers, against the world forces of this darkness, against the spiritual forces of wickedness in the heavenly places. Ephesians 6:12

Spiritual principalities work their evil schemes through *spiritual strongholds*. These are *mindsets* that exalt themselves against the knowledge of God. Well-crafted social programs can make a degree of difference, but it falls on the church to address the strongholds behind the social issues.

> For though we walk in the flesh, we do not war according to the flesh, for the weapons of our warfare are not of the flesh, but divinely powerful for the destruction of fortresses. We are destroying speculations and every lofty thing raised up against the knowledge of God, and we are taking every thought captive to the obedience of Christ, and we are ready to punish all disobedience, whenever your obedience is complete.

> You are looking at things as they are outwardly. If anyone is confident in himself that he is Christ's, let him consider this again within himself, that just as he is Christ's, so also are we. 2 Corinthians 10:3–7

Paul was referring to spiritual strongholds *within the body of Christ*. Self-conceit, it seems, was at work in their midst, and it was creating division. A community's culture will never be healthy until its churches become healthy.

How do we bring down the spiritual strongholds that corrupt communities and destroy lives? Positive change always begins at home. So, we must start within our own spheres. Thankfully, the same principles involved with preserving the unity of the church go a long way in helping to bring down spiritual strongholds.

I cannot provide statistics, but experience has shown that as the people of God learn to live out the covenantal unity of our faith, spiritual health improves. Pastors—who often suffer from isolation—build friendships. Churches also develop mindsets and practices that welcome God's life-giving kingdom.

CHANGING HEARTS THROUGH UNIFIED PRAYER

How do we confront the problems of our day? Proclaiming truth is central to the answer, but truth alone will not suffice. Cultural change requires *changed hearts*. That happens primarily through prayer—and more specifically, through *unified prayer*.

Common thought tells us that we foster change through public criticism, boycotts, protests, and the manipulation of public opinion. But these approaches tend to be rooted in a human compulsion to control. While we might win individual battles, we will lose the overall war against evil because fleshly means cannot achieve spiritual victories. *Real and lasting transformation comes only as we welcome the kingdom of God through unified prayer.*

When Jesus' disciples asked Him to teach them to pray, how did He respond? What we call "The Lord's Prayer" begins with:

"Our Father who is in heaven,
Hallowed be Your name.
Your kingdom come.
Your will be done,

On earth as it is in heaven."
Matthew 6:9b–10

How often do we recite this sacred prayer and then battle others for control? We can repeat it a million times, but efforts rooted in the human will always bear rotten fruit. Real change and genuine transformation require welcoming the kingdom of God through prayer and yielding to heaven's throne.

As much as personal prayer matters, covenants are relational and so the Bible also emphasizes *corporate* prayer. Reading through the book of Acts, we see that prayer gatherings were the norm for the early church. And how the Lord responded in miraculous ways! During that exciting season, God's people fulfilled the prophetic expectation expressed through Isaiah:

"Also the foreigners who join themselves to the Lord,
To minister to Him, and to love the name of the Lord,
To be His servants, every one who keeps from profaning the sabbath
And holds fast My covenant;
Even those I will bring to My holy mountain
And make them joyful in My house of prayer.
Their burnt offerings and their sacrifices will be acceptable on My altar;
For My house will be called a house of prayer for all the peoples."
Isaiah 56:6–7

This passage speaks of prayer among a diversity of peoples. It reflects God's passion for His entire body—not just those who share our cultures, doctrines, and practices. We naturally want to focus on ourselves, our church, or our denomination, but the Lord's vision is not nearly so narrow. Our Creator surely walks the valleys, but His vision comes from the mountaintops. If we want to see through His eyes, we must rise above our own small worlds.

I often hear devoted Christians quote 2 Chronicles 7:14: "If my people who are called by my name humble themselves, and pray and seek my face and turn from their wicked ways, then I will hear from heaven and will forgive their sin and heal their land" (ESV). This is not a message for a single person or church, but for a "people." Repentant prayer should at times be corporate because sin is so often corporate.

Jesus also alluded to the importance of unity in prayer:

> "Again I say to you, that if two of you agree on earth about anything that they may ask, it shall be done for them by My Father who is in heaven. For where two or three have gathered together in My name, I am there in their midst." Matthew 18:19–20

Throughout the Scriptures, we see the relational nature of God's heart expressed—especially regarding the unified *plurality* of the body of Christ. (I am not referring to a type of religious pluralism that would deny the core doctrines of our faith.) Many of us understand God's heart to pray *for* diverse people groups, but are we willing to pray *with* diverse people groups?

Christian unity is powerful, transforming individual churches and even denominations. But the scope of God's perspective is also much broader. To fully grasp His heart, we must think *globally* regardless of gender, skin color, nationality, or denominational affiliation. If we can learn to grow beyond our own small spheres, not only will we see the winds of positive change begin to blow, we will see the Lord continue to move for years to come.

LIFE!

What is it about praying in unity that moves the heavens? Love-based unity reflects the relationship between the Father, Son, and Holy Spirit, which is where life begins. *According to God's design, covenantal unity facilitates the impartation of life.*

When we consider the viability of a church, we might think about issues such as governance, doctrine, order of service, and style of worship. While these things are by no means unimportant, the presence of *spiritual life* is what marks the Lord's nearness.

Not every organization that professes the name of Christ reflects the reality of Christ. A church can dot every "i" and cross every "t" to perfection but still lack spiritual life. And life, we must understand, does not equate to emotional fervor. In its truest form, life involves a spiritual dynamic through which the vitality of heaven is imparted to the people of God. *Only a living church can fulfill divine purposes.*

He is the vine; we are the branches (John 15:5). Any branch that is connected to the vine will manifest the fruit thereof. If true life is present, the fruit of the Spirit will abound. When spiritual fruit (such as love, peace, patience, and kindness) is lacking, we must ask why and re-examine our connection to the vine, which also connects us to one another.

I love Psalm 133 because it reflects a greater reality regarding spiritual life:

> Behold, how good and how pleasant it is
> For brothers to dwell together in unity!
> It is like the precious oil upon the head,
> Coming down upon the beard,
> Even Aaron's beard,
> Coming down upon the edge of his robes.
> It is like the dew of Hermon
> Coming down upon the mountains of Zion;
> For there the Lord commanded the blessing—life forever.
> Psalm 133

In the eyes of heaven, Christian unity is both pleasant and refreshing. *As the Lord enjoys our covenantal oneness, He releases a powerful blessing of life into our midst.*

Whether we speak of the anointing oil of Aaron, the dew of Hermon, or the many streams that join together to make glad the city of God (Psalm 46:4), we find both joy and life through the unity of God's people. What could be more meaningful?

What do our communities need? They need spiritual strongholds to fall and spiritual life to be imparted. And nothing can accomplish these purposes like unified, faith-filled prayer.

I have found that such prayer causes the "spiritual tide" to rise in a community. Hearts soften, relationships heal, churches become healthier, and openness to the gospel increases. And the benefits are not limited to just one person or group. The entire community experiences heavenly blessings.

The principles presented in this chapter are the reason I advocate for corporate community prayer involving people from multiple churches. Unified prayer is what made the early church alive and vital. What began then continues today. Praying together with one heart and mind invites the life of heaven to triumph over the death of earth. Yes, we must work out practical dynamics to make these meetings run smoothly and effectively, but the potential blessings far surpass the effort expended.

Because of the invisible nature of the spiritual realm, it is sometimes difficult to make a direct correlation between our prayers and the specific events that take place in our communities. But over time, trends become evident, and we begin to realize the deep connection between faithful, faith-filled prayers and the transformation of community culture.

In his book, *A Gathering Momentum: Stories of Christian Unity Transforming our Towns and Cities*, Pastor Roger Sutton (the joint CEO of the Gather Movement), tells several stories of communities in the UK being deeply impacted by the efforts of churches working together. In summary, he writes:

> Over these last few decades we have seen this growing transformation, with the renewal of our

worship, our discipleship, our structures, and our mission. Although the statistics still point to decline in the UK, a substantial section of the Church is better placed than it was. We now have healthier churches, with a better grasp of what they are about and what they are seeking to do.[1]

Each story of influence presented by Sutton is unique, but a common theme transcends them all: *persistent, long-term, unified prayer.*

Many Christians in the United States think our entire past was characterized by pious and moral people faithfully attending church. And while that was true at times, there were also seasons of moral corruption and chaos. According to J. Edwin Orr in his well-researched book, *Campus Aflame*:

> Many historians have agreed that the conditions on campus and in society were deplorable. The last two decades of the eighteenth century were the darkest period, spiritually and morally, in the history of American Christianity, the low-water mark of its lowest ebb-tide, when infidelity rode roughshod over the feelings of the disoriented majority.[2]

This passage reads as though it were speaking about life in the early twenty-first century. Yes, our times are unique, but not entirely so. Orr continues, explaining the events that followed:

> In despair or hope or both, a score of New England men posted a call for a nationwide 'Concert of Prayer,' entreating the Almighty to intervene in American affairs. Ministers of every denomination joined in.

1. Roger Sutton, ed., *A Gathering Momentum: Stories of Christian Unity Transforming Our Towns and Cities* (Watford, UK: Instant Apostle, 2017), 25.
2. J. Edwin Orr, *Campus Aflame: Dynamic of Student Religious Revolution* (Glendale, CA: Regal Books, 1971), 19.

Soon reports of revivals were received from various parts of New England, and even the Maritime Provinces of Canada, throughout the Middle Atlantic States and the South, and across the mountains in the trans-Allegheny West, where phenomena beyond description were witnessed. The Second Great Awakening of American history had come. The spread of infidelity was effectively halted, and a vast new movement of benevolence began, affecting religion, philanthropy and education.[3]

What a reversal resulted from the people of God forgetting about denominational boundaries and coming together in desperate prayer for their nation! Such profound spiritual life is imparted when God's people honor and respect their covenantal unity in Christ!

Perhaps one of the most compelling examples of Christian unity comes from the Bible itself:

These [disciples of Jesus] all with one mind were continually devoting themselves to prayer, along with the women, and Mary the mother of Jesus, and with His brothers. Acts 1:14

Day by day continuing with one mind in the temple, and breaking bread from house to house, they were taking their meals together with gladness and sincerity of heart, praising God and having favor with all the people. And the Lord was adding to their number day by day those who were being saved. Acts 2:46–47

At the hands of the apostles many signs and wonders were taking place among the people; and they were all with one accord in Solomon's portico. Acts 5:12

---

3. Ibid., 20.

The book of Acts records the most dynamic time in the history of Christianity. During those years, God poured out His Holy Spirit to birth the church, thousands upon thousands came to know the Lord, and life-altering miracles abounded. All this took place within an environment of unified and persistent prayer.

Homothymadon is a key Greek word found in these passages and others in early Acts. Meaning "with one mind, by common consent, together," the word reflects well the spirit of unity that characterized the early church.[4] We might prefer to think that God has changed how He works among humans since those early, dynamic days of the church, but it would be wiser to consider how our actions differ from those of that first generation of Christians.

We are our own generation, but we, too, can pray together in faith. Jesus said He would be in the midst of only *two or three* gathered in His name (Matthew 18:19–20).

As it is with walking in love, we must *persevere* with our corporate prayers. Prayer efforts will ebb and flow; that is the nature of life in this world. But over time, positive changes will become evident. We just need to stay the course—even when it appears as though no fruit is being borne.

May our God do an amazing work of grace in our midst by knitting hearts together to persist in prayer as one body in Christ! Our world certainly needs it, and none too soon.

REFLECTION

1. Why is it necessary for hearts to be changed if cultural transformation is to take place?

2. What stands out to you about Psalm 133?

3. Please read Luke 11:1–10. What can we glean from this passage about persisting in prayer?

---

4. Barclay M. Newman Jr., *A Concise Greek-English Dictionary of the New Testament* (Stuttgart, Germany: Deutsche Bibelgesellschaft; United Bible Societies, 1993), 125.

Chapter Thirteen
On Mission

———◆———

The Lord said, "Behold, they are one people, and they all have the same language. And this is what they began to do, and now nothing which they purpose to do will be impossible for them."

Genesis 11:6

Has it ever occurred to you that one hundred pianos all tuned to the same fork are automatically tuned to each other? They are of one accord by being tuned, not to each other, but to another standard by which one must individually bow.

—A. W. Tozer

One of the apostle Paul's stronger appeals for unity can be found in his letter to the Ephesians. Examining the nature of this letter, we realize that it was not written to a simple house church, but to a larger group of believers, if not the church universal. God's emphasis on the church is never just about "our" church.

I therefore, a prisoner for the Lord, urge you to walk in a manner worthy of the calling to which you have been called, with all humility and gentleness, with patience, bearing with one another in love, eager to maintain the unity of the Spirit in the bond of peace. There is one body and one Spirit—just as you were

> called to the one hope that belongs to your call— one Lord, one faith, one baptism, one God and Father of all, who is over all and through all and in all. Ephesians 4:1–6 (ESV)

In 1 Corinthians 12:12–27, Paul also celebrates the church as the *body of Christ* in which each member plays a vital part. So often, we tend to think in terms of a particular church or denomination, when a broader perspective is warranted.

I once watched a white-tailed deer reach forward with a rear hoof to scratch an itch behind its ear. What did that peculiar scene tell me? A body part reveals its connection to the head by how it works with the other members of the body. *If we proclaim ourselves to be connected to Christ as the head of the church, our ability to work with other members of His body should bear witness.*

Multiple Christian churches collectively form the body of Christ in a community. One congregation might emphasize outreach, another family education, and still another, community service. And while our pride often lauds our approach as superior to others', the Lord intends that we *complement* one another in fulfilling His plans and purposes for that area.

THE GREAT COMMISSION

As children of God and citizens of His kingdom, our primary loyalty lies with the King of Glory. And since the mindsets of this world conflict with His (Isaiah 55:6–9), the Bible regards us as strangers and aliens on earth (1 Peter 2:11). At the same time, our Lord has always intended for His people to bless others. This intention is expressed in God's call to Abraham, and then in many other places throughout Scripture.

> Now the Lord said to Abram, "Go from your country and your kindred and your father's house to the land that I will show you. And I will make of you a great

nation, and I will bless you and make your name great, so that you will be a blessing. I will bless those who bless you, and him who dishonors you I will curse, and in you all the families of the earth shall be blessed." Genesis 12:1–3 (ESV)

Many centuries later, as the people of Israel processed the shock of their exile into Babylon, the Lord sent them a vital message through the prophet Jeremiah:

"Build houses and live in them; and plant gardens and eat their produce. Take wives and become the fathers of sons and daughters, and take wives for your sons and give your daughters to husbands, that they may bear sons and daughters; and multiply there and do not decrease. Seek the welfare of the city where I have sent you into exile, and pray to the Lord on its behalf; for in its welfare you will have welfare." Jeremiah 29:5–7

Yes, we are called to be separate from the world in the sense of holiness. But if our God commanded the exiles of Babylon (consider the example set by Daniel and his friends) to invest in that idolatrous nation with all its heinous acts, how much more should we care for and about our communities?

As much as we need healthy relationships with our brothers and sisters in Christ, and as much as our unity matters within itself, we are also united by a common mission. *Our fractured and dying world desperately needs a unified church to rise.*

If the idolatrous people of Shinar held so much potential in their unity, how much more the people of God? And how this lost and broken world needs what a unified church has to offer!

Those without Christ are spiritually lost, and modern technology is not making them any more "found." There will always be hard and obstinate people who reject God, but many more are broken and desperate for hope and meaning in life. The church has what the world needs, but we do not always represent Christ well. How many souls would be saved from the curse of sin and death if more Christians actually reflected the teachings of Jesus by loving one another and advancing His purposes together?

How strange it must seem in the eyes of heaven that multiple congregations within a community would compete and criticize one another while trying to accomplish the same purposes! If nothing else, we are unified by our mission.

> And Jesus came up and spoke to them [His disciples], saying, "All authority in heaven and on earth has been given to Me. Go, therefore, and make disciples of all the nations, baptizing them in the name of the Father and the Son and the Holy Spirit, teaching them to follow all that I commanded you; and behold, I am with you always, to the end of the age." Matthew 28:18–20 (NASB)

The Great Commission is central to the purpose of the church, and it is a task so great that we can accomplish it only together.

In many ways, fulfilling the Great Commission involves a difficult and dangerous "rescue effort" with multiple parties working together in unison. During a natural disaster, people who might not get along otherwise choose to do so because human lives are at stake. If we can easily grasp such a need for cooperative efforts in our natural world, why do we so often turn a blind eye regarding spiritual matters? Effectively reaching the world for Jesus can be done only together and in cooperation with one another.

Friends of mine raise funds and are employed through Elim Fellowship—our ministry organization—but they work through two different international mission organizations. These groups, comprised of staff from multiple nations, reach and serve people in some of the most difficult environments in our world. I find the unified approach refreshing because no one cares about getting credit, only fulfilling God's purposes. How I wish this type of approach were the norm and not the exception! How many more people could we reach by working together? *Unity is more than an ideal; it is life for those who need the touch of our Savior.*

Beyond the Great Commission, we must also consider our overall influence on the world around us. As much as the Great Commission centers on the gospel of our Lord, it also encompasses blessing the *whole* person—something a divided kingdom cannot do effectively. Only together can we wield the influence needed to transform our neighborhoods, cities, and even nations. The need is dire, and we cannot allow room for petty pride.

A VISION FOR THE FUTURE

A unified church might seem rare, yet it is not beyond reach. Even today, the Lord works powerfully through Christian unity. But the scope needs to increase if we are to fulfill His purposes. How many souls on this planet are lost without God? How many have never heard the name of Jesus Christ? How many young people end their lives due to hopelessness? Do we care enough to work together for the cause of the gospel? Certainly, the size of the task is beyond any one church, denomination, or ministry stream.

Can you envision churches joining together to pray for their community? Can you picture pastors sharing ideas and creating strategic plans to meet needs and bless families? Can you imagine exasperated government officials and educators turning to church leaders for help because they share a common concern and are a pleasure to work with? Can you see families being restored, criminals redeemed, and cycles of poverty broken?

Too often, our worlds are too small and our vision too limited. Again, our Lord is not the God of just a few, but a multitude. His love for people runs deep, and He has strategically placed Christians throughout a broad spectrum of society. Within our churches are gifted and passionate individuals who deeply care about those around them. Are we providing them with opportunities to make a difference beyond the walls of our church buildings?

Such service can include—but need not be limited to—political action. Indeed, the Lord calls people to influence politics, but the vision for His kingdom coming to earth far exceeds what can be accomplished by imperfect politicians who so often use divisive means to accomplish their goals. Political action bears good fruit only as we live by kingdom principles.

If our focus for bringing change to our communities is primarily political, we will endure endless frustration and likely become hardened. Moreover, the divisive nature of political maneuvering will drain our vitality. But working together as the body of Christ to serve in a variety of ways, we can find joy, rich relationships, and countless opportunities to provide witness for the King we so dearly love.

As the children of God, we are bound together by a sacred covenant. Regardless of our political affiliation or denominational connection, we are brothers and sisters in Christ. Your success is my success, and my failure is your failure. In the end, what matters most is that we glorify God not just through our words, but also through actions that reflect the love of Christ. If we truly care about God's passions, if we truly care about our communities, and if we truly care about fulfilling the Great Commission, we will learn to work and pray together with other members of Christ's body.

REFLECTION

1. Think about the churches in your community. In what ways do they complement each other?

2. How does our unity—or lack thereof—affect our ability to fulfill the Great Commission?

3. Allow yourself to dream for a minute. What would it be like if the churches in your community worked together? What can you envision them accomplishing?

CHAPTER FOURTEEN
GOD'S GLORIOUS CHURCH

—————◆—————

Husbands, love your wives, just as Christ also loved the church and gave Himself up for her, so that He might sanctify her, having cleansed her by the washing of water with the word, that He might present to Himself the church in all her glory, having no spot or wrinkle or any such thing; but that she would be holy and blameless.

Ephesians 5:25–27

The unity of Christendom is not a luxury, but a necessity. The World will go limping until Christ's prayer that all may be one is answered. We must have unity, not at all costs, but at all risks. A unified Church is the only offering we dare present to the coming Christ, for in it alone will He find room to dwell.

—Charles Brent

What does it mean for the church to be without "spot or wrinkle"? At least in part, our perspective relates to our understanding of *righteousness*. In the Old Testament era, before the people of Israel endured a harsh captivity in Babylon, righteousness seemed to be defined by a relational element. To be righteous was to do right by the Lord and humanity—especially the covenant family of God.

Throughout the centuries, Israel struggled to stay loyal to God, often embracing the idolatrous practices of the surrounding nations. After the death of Alexander the Great in 323 BC, Greek leaders began forcing the Israelites to adopt their customs. Out of this tumultuous season, a group of religious leaders (called the Pharisees) exhorted the people to stay true to their Jewish faith. Somewhere in the process, they lost sight of God's relational intent.

When Jesus came on the scene, He chastised the Pharisees for caring more about rituals and laws than the well-being of people. Contending for truth while ignoring the centrality of love misses the mark of God's design. The apostle Paul reminds us:

> But the goal of our instruction is love from a pure heart and a good conscience and a sincere faith.
> 1 Timothy 1:5

The Pharisees sought to honor God but missed His intent because of their rigid adherence to Jewish traditions. They failed to understand that, at its core, the Mosaic law was about *love*.

> Owe nothing to anyone except to love one another; for he who loves his neighbor has fulfilled the law. For this, "You shall not commit adultery, You shall not murder, You shall not steal, You shall not covet," and if there is any other commandment, it is summed up in this saying, "You shall love your neighbor as yourself." Love does no wrong to a neighbor; therefore love is the fulfillment of the law. Romans 13:8–10

Christianity is a covenantal belief system in which relationships are sacred. In particular, we can speak of two enduring covenants that have been established by God Himself: *the marriage covenant* and *the new covenant in Christ*. While we no longer seek to be righteous by trying to live up to law-based standards, the Lord still calls us to faithfully elevate covenantal love. This is not a love of our own definition, but one established by the sovereign King of Glory. Those who stray from honoring the covenants do so at great peril.

How easy it is to miss the heart of the Lord's commandments by justifying judgmental thoughts toward other believers in the name of righteousness. We dare not negate the importance of moral purity, but rather recognize that its roots stem from a covenantal love that has been designed and defined by our Creator.

A LIVING TEMPLE

The Lord's grand plans for His people will always entail a relational element. Together, God is building us into a *living temple*—one that is worthy of His presence:

> And coming to Him as to a living stone which has been rejected by men, but is choice and precious in the sight of God, you also, as living stones, are being built up as a spiritual house for a holy priesthood, to offer up spiritual sacrifices acceptable to God through Jesus Christ. 1 Peter 2:4–5

Temples exist for worship and sacred sacrifice. Neither will be fully realized until God's people grasp His heart for unity and display His glory by joining together through the perfect bond of love.

Christians from various streams are interwoven with one another as *living stones* in the holy temple of God. When one succeeds, all succeed. When one fails, all fail. How much would the fabric of today's church change if we all understood and valued the dynamics of our Lord's design?

THE VICTORIOUS CHURCH

Consider, for a minute, how the church came into existence. An unlikely Messiah trained a ragtag band of unlikely disciples, only to be crucified on a wooden cross by the authorities who ruled and reigned over human affairs. The death of the carpenter's son should have been the end of the story, but in so many ways, it was only the beginning.

Fifty days after Christ's resurrection, the church was birthed as God poured out His Spirit on people of diverse nations and tongues. Against all odds, the church that prayed with one heart and mind grew to triumph over one of the greatest empires of all time.

Unfortunately, the momentum did not last. Factions formed and leadership became political. Christians adopted the ways of the world instead of embracing the mindset of God's kingdom. Corruption and decay then undermined the cultural influence built by a more vibrant church. Thankfully, this was not the end of the story!

Over the past several centuries, the Lord has been drawing the church back to His original intent. The process has not been seamless—we have seen plenty of human failures along the way— but His work persists nonetheless. And if there is one thing we can say about the God who created us, it is that He never fails to accomplish what He purposes to do.

While the church has stagnated in much of the West, it continues to grow rapidly in many developing countries. Today, light is triumphing over darkness in what were once the darkest reaches of the globe.

Westerners see mainly the struggle and the decline of spiritual life. But there is much more to that story as well. Vibrant, healthy, life-giving churches are growing and touching lives in the West even as many other congregations decline.

What encourages me most, though, is not what I see, but what I read in the Bible. *Jesus is not coming back for a divided, defeated church. He is returning for a unified, victorious bride without spot or blemish.* And while there are many obvious failures among Christians today, our Lord is raising up a body of people who will triumph over darkness by bearing abundant spiritual fruit.

Jesus established the new covenant with His blood. That includes our salvation but also more than our salvation. As much as forgiveness matters, we are not saved just to be forgiven. We are the Royal Family of God that has been redeemed at a great price. Our honored status will one day be revealed to all, but for now we display our Father's glory by loving one another as a family should.

Hardness, bitterness, and judgmentalism will have no sway over God's children in the last days. Instead, light, life, and love will mark those abiding in the eternal vine as the *covenant family* of God. Do not lose heart! Our eternal King will be glorified and the greatness of His glory revealed in due season.

CLOSING THOUGHTS

We have covered a lot of ground in this little book. I shared about my story and how the Lord dealt with my motives for ministry. We explored why unity matters and what it means to our Lord. We also addressed the challenges of navigating doctrinal differences and dealing with false prophets. Finally, we got a taste of what God wants to do in our day through the unity of His people.

What has the Lord spoken to your heart throughout your reading? Do you need to make adjustments to your attitude? Fall on your face in repentance? Redeem your tongue? Begin tearing down walls and building bridges? Perhaps you are thinking of a relationship that needs to be reconciled. Or maybe you feel it is time to join—or even help start—a community prayer meeting.

Perhaps the ideals I have presented resonate with your heart, but you know they will create problems with others in your organizational sphere. Your movement might routinely criticize those with different practices and doctrinal positions. You know that if you break course, you will be criticized yourself—and perhaps even ostracized. But is that not how we initiate positive change? The human will is a strange creature. Often, it must be challenged before new ideas are accepted.

Microwave ovens are common in US households today, but that has not always been the case. When they first became available to the general public, microwaves were a novelty. To purchase one, a person had to go to a department store and talk with a sales representative. In our early years of marriage, before we had kids, Debi and I would buy a major household item each Christmas. One year, that item was a microwave. (Alas, I reveal my age!)

As we enjoyed our new oven—aside from the stone-hard pierogies of our first cooking attempt—I asked my wife when she was going to tell her parents about the purchase. "I'm not," Debi replied. "They'll just say, 'What did you do that for? You don't need one of those!'"

Newly married and thinking she should handle things differently, I encouraged Debi to tell her mom and dad about the microwave. My wife reluctantly did so, and they responded exactly as she had said they would. A few years later, however, her parents purchased a microwave oven of their own!

Change can be difficult—especially as we grow older and become more set in our ways. But positive change will never happen if we are not challenged by the examples of others. For those who esteem the Scriptures, Christian unity should be the norm and not the exception. But to get to that place, faithful believers must patiently blaze the trail by setting an example and appealing to our collective love for the Lord.

We do not know what God will do in response to our efforts, but we do know that our King never fails. In spite of our past failures and disappointments, I am excited to see what good things await the Royal Family of God. It is time to put the old, dark ways behind us and step into the light of God's glorious love—together!

REFLECTION

1. How do you see the Lord beautifying His bride, the church?

2. What does 1 Peter 2:4–5 mean to you?

3. What next step is the Lord calling you to take regarding the unity of His church?

Practical Thoughts About Community Prayer

"Again I say to you, that if two of you agree on earth about anything that they may ask, it shall be done for them by My Father who is in heaven. For where two or three have gathered together in My name, I am there in their midst."

Matthew 18:19–20

There has never been a spiritual awakening in any country or locality that did not begin in united prayer.

—A. T. Pierson

This book is not a comprehensive document, and I cannot provide you with specific answers to all your "how to" questions. I can, however, spur your thinking, and hopefully awaken a passion that has been simmering deep within your soul.

Generating interest in community prayer has exciting potential, but the effort requires the patience of Job. Two specific elements work together to create a powerful mix. They involve prayer initiatives combined with ongoing "routine" efforts.

Prayer initiatives draw Christians together and create momentum. Simply asking or encouraging people to pray will often get a minimal response. Holding a time-sensitive initiative or event, on the other hand, can provide big benefits.

Prayer initiatives are best timed to coincide with the cycles of everyday living. The beginning of a new year is probably the most effective because people are naturally ready for a fresh start. In fact, many want to put the old year behind them, which means they are more open to new ideas. And, of course, many churches begin the new year with a season of fasting and prayer. Initiatives can also be started around Easter and at the beginning of a school year, but these seasons are often busier for people than the beginning of the year.

The most effective initiatives have the support of a church's lead pastor. If the pastor is not committed to the effort, the lack of enthusiasm will be evident. Announcing the initiative from the pulpit over the course of several weeks will help maximize congregational response. Preaching about prayer and unity will take things even further. At the very minimum, all materials—as well as planned events—should obtain pastoral approval beforehand.

If you launch an initiative, you will want to communicate frequently and effectively. Well-designed resources such as printed materials, websites, emails, and texts will prove helpful. The *Community Prayer Devotional* I wrote is designed for a 30-day initiative that can be followed by a community-wide event. Digital copies of the devotional can be downloaded at no cost from our website (sfme.org). Other organizations also provide prayer resources of this type. The most important thing is to find an approach that works best for you and your community.

Our first local initiative ran for the first thirty days of January and utilized my devotional. For those who signed up, we also sent out an automated daily email with prayer points. Those efforts worked well and generated considerable enthusiasm among the participating churches.

As the initiative progressed, we announced a community prayer meeting to be held at one of our local churches. The response was excellent, with a nice turnout for our rural community. We provided an outline of basic prayer concerns—such as the educational system, government entities, and local business leaders—for that meeting.

We did make a mistake, however, by using an open mic system, which allowed anyone to pray for all to hear. Sadly, some people just want a public voice, while others might lack situational awareness. That first effort did not go poorly by any means, but we also recognized that adjustments were warranted.

Two approaches seemed to work especially well. The first was to have one or several pastors lead the people in prayer. The other, which I liked best, was to divide those attending into small groups of 4–6 people. A leader would introduce the topic, give the groups several minutes to pray, and then end with a prayer to close out the topic. Again, you will want to find an approach that works best for your community.

Trying to be as consistent as possible, we began to meet monthly at different churches within the community. We chose monthly meetings because we wanted our efforts to be sustainable. If we attempt too much in our enthusiasm, people will become overwhelmed and cease their involvement.

Over time, the number attending dwindled a bit, but the meetings remained vibrant. Then the Covid-19 pandemic hit. We lost momentum, but thankfully, our efforts were not entirely derailed. Scheduling prayer walks in nice weather added variety and proved effective in keeping our monthly meetings going. In fact, prayer walks became common practice during the summers.

Continuing monthly prayer meetings over a span of several years is not an easy task. They must remain a deliberate and steady point of conversation among leaders, and expectations must be relaxed regarding the participation of any one person or church.

One of the great dangers with these types of efforts involves "keeping score" of who does what. The best thing we can do is continue to communicate, give thanks for whoever attends, and stay the course through the ebbs and flows of life. Otherwise, levels of judgment and guilt rise while morale sinks.

Over time, our monthly prayer meetings evolved to a core group of people who loved to pray. Each meeting was different, and

I am happy to say we never had a bad one. In one way or another, we always experienced a touch from heaven as the Lord flooded us with His life.

Another challenge we face in promoting prayer involves the difficulty of establishing a clear link between our prayers and God's answers. Who can say for sure that a new kingdom-minded pastor coming into our community was a direct answer to our prayers? Or that a life was spared from a tragic end because of our efforts? Surely, the ability to measure the effects of prayer is beyond our means. Even so, sharing testimonies of God at work will strengthen faith and encourage people to press in with their prayers.

We can also sense when the spiritual tide begins to rise. It does not take a rocket scientist to connect the dots when people outside the community start asking what is going on (in a good way). We can also take heart when we hear reports of high school and college students not only becoming more open to the gospel, but also getting actively involved with local ministries.

Above all, though, *we believe*. We continue to stand on the promises of God's Word, and we avail ourselves faithful to pray according to His desires. Yes, we have much to learn along the way, and the results are often beyond our ability to measure. But nothing brings heaven's glory to earth like the power of unified prayer!

Our Lord never hesitates to call His people to achieve the impossible. From the Hebrews 11 heroes of our faith, to a multitude of unlikely champions since, He has used passionate and faithful men and women to transform nations. Will you embrace the vision? Will you join with others to persist in faith, love, and prayer? This book has come to its necessary end, but there can be so much more to your story as you faithfully pray and honor the Royal Family of God!

ACKNOWLEDGMENT

Every book I write requires a collaborative effort involving wonderful people who hold tight a vision to serve beyond themselves. And I never cease to be amazed by the way each unique contribution helps improve the quality of my work. In this case, I would like to thank Ken Cramer, Deb Croyle, Ryan Faison, K-Lee Gaffney, Stan Grant, Jeff Hill, Robb Horner, Jason Hutchins, Bob Jeannot, Lynn Johnson, Jackie Kuehn, Lynda Logue, David Ludwig, Mel Masengale, Samantha Mitchell, Elaine Rice, Keith Rowell, Debi Santos, Paula Saylor, Rob Sparr, Todd Stanley, and Judah Thomas for their awesome contributions to this work.

I am also deeply appreciative of those who empower me to write life-changing books by supporting our ministry efforts. Our readers might not know their names, but heaven surely does!

About the Author

Bob Santos writes to see lives transformed by God's goodness. Years of working in college ministry revealed that people crave to know more about God not only in their hearts through faith, but also through a deeper understanding of the truths found in His Word.

Pursuing spiritual vitality, Bob helps others "connect the dots" of Biblical truth by addressing "missing links" of contemporary theology. In this, Bob's books and video teachings explore key Biblical themes—such as covenants, grace, identity, rest, unity, and wisdom—that are often misunderstood or widely ignored. His explanations of difficult concepts, combined with inspirational messages of hope in Christ, are insightful, thought-provoking, and transformational as they explore the Christian faith in an understandable and yet intellectually satisfying way.

Bob was licensed for Christian ministry in 1997 and ordained in 2005 through Elim Fellowship (www.elimfellowship.org). In 2006, Bob and his wife Debi founded Search for Me Ministries, Inc. (sfme.org) with the mission to help form and equip a generation of world changers for Christ through the production of Biblically based teaching resources.

College sweethearts, Bob and Debi have been married for nearly forty years. Together, they have two adult children, one grandchild, and three granddogs. When he is not writing, speaking, or leading a Bible study, you will likely find Bob doing something in the great outdoors.

Additional Books from
Search for Me Ministries

Paperback copies of *Greater Glory: The Transformational Power of Christian Unity* (also available as an audiobook) can be purchased through major online retailers. Volume discounts are available through SfMe Ministries (sfme.org) for ministry organizations.

There is a profound logic behind all that God does, but it is not human logic. *The Age of Abiding: Experiencing the Life of the Vine* provides powerful insights into human nature, helping the reader better grasp the mysterious beauty of the Christian gospel. (Audiobook available.)

The Search for Rest: Fifty Days to a More Peaceful Life provides an awesome personal or group study that explores the concept of the Sabbath from both spiritual and physical perspectives. This thought-provoking book meets a powerful need in a world that is filled with anxiety and unrest. (Audiobook available.)

Much of the Christian faith makes little sense to the modern, Western mind because the Bible was written with a mentality that differs from current thought. *Drinking Truth: Embracing the Covenant Mindset of the Bible* provides an insightful look at the new covenant in light of the covenantal mindset with which the Bible was penned. (Audiobook available.)

The *Community Prayer Devotional* is a powerful book that brings churches together to pray. Even better, the cover can be personalized to fit your community, allowing people to take ownership and embrace prayer as a lifestyle! (Audiobook available.)

If you want to gain a Biblical perspective on identity, *From Glory to Glory: Finding Real Significance in an Image-Driven World* is the book for you! Not only is this powerful forty-day devotional filled with illuminating insights, it will also help to renew your mind as a beloved child of the King of Glory. (Audiobook available.)

Say Goodbye to Regret: Discovering the Secret to a Blessed Life is a life-changing book that deals with the problem of regret on two fronts. Learn how to move beyond the lingering pain of regret and also how to avoid regrets entirely by pursuing the rich treasures of God's spiritual wisdom. (Audiobook available.)

The TouchPoint: Connecting with God through the Bible is a valuable resource for those who are interested in learning more about the Bible. Revised in 2020, this book provides a great introduction to the Christian Scriptures while emphasizing a personal relationship with God. (Audiobook available.)

The Divine Progression of Grace: Blazing a Trail to Fruitful Living thoughtfully explores God's grace from a perspective of empowerment as well as acceptance. This book will take you deeper into a relationship with your Creator and also help make you more usable for His purposes.

Each reading in *Champions in the Wilderness: Fifty-Two Devotions to Guide and Strengthen Emerging Overcomers* draws from a deep well of truth to encourage, strengthen, and instruct those who desire to walk with God but are struggling in the face of adversity. The format of this devotional lends itself well to group discussion. (Audiobook available.)

Posting Book Reviews

Please consider posting an online review of this book. Honest reviews are deeply appreciated and provide an easy way for our readers to contribute to our ministry efforts. Also, if your life has been touched by one of our resources, please recommend it to others.

SfMe Media

SfMe Media is a division of Search for Me Ministries, Inc. (SfMe Ministries)—an IRS-recognized 501(c)(3) nonprofit organization. Search for Me Ministries burns with a vision to help form and equip a generation of world changers for Christ. We believe in the importance of reaching those who do not know the Lord, but we also recognize the need for healthy churches as landing places for new believers. By helping Christians grow to maturity with our uniquely flavored teaching resources, we are helping to create environments that foster the fulfilment of the Great Commission in every way.